OPERATION *SPLINTER FACTOR*

OPERATION
SPLINTER FACTOR

by STEWART STEVEN

J. B. LIPPINCOTT COMPANY
Philadelphia and New York

U.S. Library of Congress Cataloging in Publication Data

Steven, Stewart, birth date
  Operation splinter factor.

  Bibliography: p.
  1. Subversive activities—Europe, Eastern.
2. Europe, Eastern—Politics. 3. United States.
Central Intelligence Agency. I. Title.
DR48.5.S77   327′.12′0947   73-22353
ISBN-0-397-00982-8

FOR INKA, FOREVER

CONTENTS

Operation Splinter Factor represents the nadir of American foreign-policy making during those bleak Cold War years. It degraded the cause which it set out to serve and set back the possibility of *détente* between East and West for a generation.

What is perhaps even more shocking is that by its own standards it must be judged a failure, and that accordingly all of the human lives which it destroyed were destroyed in vain. For the plain fact is that not only did Operation Splinter Factor not achieve what it set out to achieve, but it did not contribute in any sense to the well-being of the peoples of the Western world which the authors of this plan were pledged to serve. Worse still, it never could have worked, for it was an operation based upon ignorance and fear—politically and philosophically unfounded.

The story of this clandestine intelligence operation has been pieced together from a variety of sources over a period of two years and sets out to re-create as accurately as possible what was probably the foremost intelligence battle of the Cold War.

I have employed all of the journalistic techniques I know in establishing the material, operating in an area

where facts are spread thinly over a ground covered with
half-truths and lies. Necessarily I have had to rely on
verbal evidence; documents and files are simply not available. If we believe that contemporary history must be told
on the basis of documentary evidence before it becomes
creditable, then we must also accept that everything will
either be written with the government's seal of approval or
not be written at all. We certainly would have to accept
that no book about modern intelligence operations or
about any of our secret services should ever be attempted,
for no files worth having will ever be disclosed. It is a situation with which I'm accustomed.

Very rarely, during my journalistic career as a West-
minster-based political correspondent, or as a diplomatic
correspondent and later foreign editor of a major British
newspaper, have I found it possible to base politically sensitive stories upon documents. Journalists looking for disclo-
sures operate in a world where the best one can hope for is
a whispered confidence or a betrayal of some dark secret by
a disaffected government employee. At a time when more
and more government business appears to be conducted in
the open, though less and less is actually revealed, this
approach is the only way we have of carrying out our primary duty of informing the public. Getting over the foot-
lights, easing away the scenery and peeping backstage,
where the real work is being done—as distinct from the
technicolor illusion which is delighting the audience—is
my kind of journalism. *Operation Splinter Factor* is that
kind of book.

One cannot, however, write about a political intelligence operation without becoming incensed by the knowledge that under current regulations the material with
which one is dealing will never be made available to historians. The role of political intelligence in the postwar world

is really quite enormous. Occasional crass failures like the Bay of Pigs operation come under public scrutiny (though I suspect still more remains concealed), but by and large we know nothing about the real work being done by the intelligence agencies on our behalf.

Leaving aside the Communist world, I cannot believe that the political and moral health of the Western world is best served by the ability of our intelligence agencies to escape all public accountability either now or in the future. State Department, Foreign Office, presidential and prime ministerial papers will eventually be available to the historians. The files of the Central Intelligence Agency and the Secret Intelligence Service, to name but two secret agencies, will be locked away forever. A major campaign which will force an end to this unhappy state of affairs needs to be launched immediately. It is pure sophistry to suggest that the security of the state will be imperiled if, after seventy-five years, say, the secret archives of government are opened up. If now we were to know the dread truth about the year 1899, would anything but the reputations of some of our long-dead leaders seriously suffer? Looking to the future, can one really believe that a historian writing about the Vietnam War will really understand that issue without reading every document on that subject in the files of the CIA? Will an Englishman ever properly understand Ulster without perusing the files of Special Branch and SIS? Will anyone understand the era in which we live without putting under the microscope those agencies which have done so much to shape it?

This book provides one small glimpse.

Stewart Steven

ACKNOWLEDGMENTS

Although many of the people who assisted me must remain anonymous, I would like to thank the staffs of Radio Free Europe in Munich and New York, who gave me access to their archives.

I am grateful to the staffs of various Congressional committees, especially to the members of the House Committee on Internal Security, who gave me their valuable time as well as a desk at which to work while going through their records. The staffs of the Library of Congress, the New York Public Library and the London Library were all extremely helpful and courteous. Thanks to Dr. Howard Gottlieb, associate director for the Division of Special Collections at Boston University's Mugar Library, I found the papers of Flora Lewis, who generously permitted me to consult her voluminous research notes.

I was fortunate in having the assistance of my wife, Inka, who speaks and reads Russian and Polish fluently. Though not a journalist, she did, in fact, evolve into a fine reporter and, on a solo trip to Munich on my behalf, produced material in a few days which I had spent months trying to track down.

Ross Mark, the distinguished Washington correspondent of the London *Daily Express*, gave me much assistance in Washington. Mrs. Heather Dyer did a splendid job in typing the manuscript, and my son, Jack, managed to be a tower of strength during the arduous months I was at home writing. Mrs. Barrie Van Dyck of J. B. Lippincott proved to be a superb and understanding editor, and I am grateful to her for the hard work she put into this book.

Above all, I am indebted to that fine American journalist and historian Ladislas Farago, who was in on the earliest days of the CIA and was a member of the Central Intelligence Group which preceded it. He was an invaluable source of detailed information, and without his counsel as well as his friendship, which I value most highly, this book could not have been written.

To them all—the many people in America, in Britain and in several European countries who gave me their help and guidance—I owe much.

"Now, as nearly as I can make out, those fellows in the CIA don't just report on wars and the like, they go out and make their own, and there's nobody to keep track of what they're up to. They spend billions of dollars on stirring up trouble so they'll have something to report on. . . . It's become a government all of its own and all secret. They don't have to account to anybody.

"That's a very dangerous thing in a democratic society. . . ."

—Harry S. Truman
Quoted by Merle Miller in
Plain Speaking (Berkley/Putnam's)

PROLOGUE

The year was 1947. Arbitrarily and cruelly the world had been cut in two. On one side was Communist Russia and her newly acquired Eastern European allies, seeking to export militant Marxism throughout the world in order to maintain the inviolability of her own revolution. On the other side was the United States of America and her Western European friends, fearful of communism, strong and yet never quite strong enough. In the East there were the peoples' democracies; in the West our democratic way of life. Words had lost all meaning, and the late 1940's was an insane era.

In previous ages the unbearable tension would eventually have been relieved by the purgative of war, but now that option was closed. Europe barely survived the war that had just been; it would not survive a nuclear conflict.

Thus, deprived of that time-honored method of resolving irreconcilable differences, these two mighty blocs spat hate like two fighting cocks not yet released from their cages. Each made terrible errors in judgment; each befouled the atmosphere with hysterical polemics and propaganda; and each was responsible in full measure for the rigors of what quickly became known as the Cold War—a state of hostile nonhostility which haunts us to this day.

The West believed that freedom and all that it stood for was at stake in the fight, but the East's point of view was unclear to most people at that time. During those years the Soviet Union and the satellite countries felt considerably more threatened by war than did the West. The West had the bomb, and the majority of East European leaders believed she would use it. It had already become an article of faith that the Americans had dropped it on Hiroshima and Nagasaki not primarily to defeat the Japanese but to impress the Russians, who knew—because negotiations were being conducted through them—the Japanese were on the verge of unconditional surrender when the bomb was dropped. So to the Russians, every act of theirs which cut across Western interests was a defensive rather than an aggressive measure.

This is not to say that Stalin was a benevolent old gentleman. He was involved in big-power politics. He saw the tidemark across the face of Europe where the Red Army came to rest at the end of World War II as the outer fringes of his new territory. The Americans, he assumed, took a similar position. Thus, just as Poland had to be absorbed into the empire merely because of her proximity to the Soviet Union, though her political traditions were demonstrably at the other end of the spectrum, so France would be absorbed into the Western camp, though the Communists were the strongest and most disciplined of all

French political parties to emerge from the war. The Potsdam Treaty, Stalin believed, permitted the Russians, the British and the Americans to carve up the world among them. It may have been a crude point of view, but certainly the treaty as well as wartime conversations he had with Churchill and Roosevelt encouraged this belief.*

Stalin's policies in fact were purely czarist in ideology and execution. The Baltic States were to be absorbed in the Soviet Union; Poland's eastern frontiers were clawed back into Russia proper while the rest of the country became a vassal state. He put pressure on Persia, Manchuria, the frontier provinces of Turkey and the Dardanelles. The dream of a Mediterranean warm-water port was once more revived when he asked for the trusteeship of Libya. He was Peter the Great incarnate.

Against that background one can see that he would regard the Truman Doctrine of March 1947 as being a brutal threat to the Soviet Union and its legitimate aspirations. The abandonment of America's traditional isolationism was to any Marxist historian sufficient proof that America's foreign policy was ultimately aggressive in nature. To a czarist like Stalin, it had even more shocking implications. An entirely new continental political and military leadership had emerged, seemingly from nowhere, to upset every single preconception about the balance of

---

* At Potsdam and at Yalta, and at unilateral agreements between the various parties, Roosevelt, Churchill and Stalin proceeded, like settlers in the old West, to divide up the known world among them. Perhaps the most incredible example of this was the agreement between Churchill and Stalin to divide the Balkans—what Churchill described as "our affairs in the Balkans." The Soviets were to receive 80 percent influence in Bulgaria, 90 percent in Rumania, 80 percent in Hungary, and share responsibility with Britain in Yugoslavia; the British received 90 percent responsibility for Greece. As Churchill subsequently wrote: " . . . quite naturally Soviet Russia has vital interests in the countries bordering on the Black Sea, by one of whom, Rumania, she has been wantonly attacked with twenty-six divisions, and with the other of whom, Bulgaria, she has ancient ties."

power in Europe. To him this was as unacceptable and potentially dangerous as it was to America when several years later Russia used Cuba to seek to establish a bridgehead in the Western hemisphere.

A nonpropagandist view of postwar history now would have to acknowledge that when Stalin forced Czechoslovakia to reject the Marshall Plan in June of 1947, he was reacting to events rather than initiating them. As far as he was concerned, the West had drawn the lines of demarcation fairly clearly only forty-eight hours earlier, when all Communists in the French and Italian governments were summarily dismissed. That was the sort of activity he could well understand. No one could complain, he reasoned, if he adopted similar measures behind his front gate.

It is at least arguable—though it is perhaps not yet respectable to do so—that the intensification of Communist control over Eastern Europe was the consequence rather than the cause of the breakdown of relations between the two great powers. The fault lies not only with Joseph Stalin but also with the West's refusal to accept Russia's legitimate security arrangements in Eastern Europe.

It was conveniently ignored at the time that Russia and her Eastern dominions had rather more to fear from an outbreak of renewed fighting than anyone else. Their war had indeed been a frightful thing. In the Warsaw uprising the Poles lost more dead than the Americans did throughout the entire war. The Russians lost more in the war than all of the Western nations put together. Twenty million Russians perished. Whole cities were razed. By comparison, Western nations had a very comfortable time, and to the East Europeans it was somewhat sickening to observe how quickly the West was prepared to regard the Western zones of Germany as a bulwark against the "Red hordes."

Russia's problems were intensified by the inexperience

and often the plain unsuitability of the men who came to power in Eastern Europe after the war. Revolutions tend to produce too many revolutionaries and too few leaders. That complex psychological mix which induces a person to give up health, wealth, prospects and even his life in order to work and fight for an illegal, underground organization is rarely found in a person with the qualities required to run an efficient, modern state. And most of the East European leaders, if not all, were precisely of that type; they had spent a lifetime of illegal activity fighting for a cause which, if the war had not intervened, was doomed in most cases to failure. Many had spent years in prisons or concentration camps. Some had been forced to flee to Russia in the thirties. Others had joined the International Brigade in Spain. Many, once war broke out, fought valiantly for the Allies in resistance movements, which existed in every country in Europe. They may often have been wrongheaded but they were all a remarkable breed.

When they all came back from the war to take the reward so abundantly and so clearly due them, the stresses and strains of their respective experiences began to tell. Those who had fought in the war felt that those who had sat it out in Moscow were mere parlor Communists—men who had taken the easy option. The Muscovites regarded the Internationalists as aliens—men who had been irreparably softened by constant access to bourgeois ideology.

The intensification of the Cold War turned these suspicions into bitter and often horrible enmities. To the Muscovites, a closer alliance with the Soviet Union appeared to be the only salvation of their nations and their beliefs against the threat of attack from the West. While never really dissenting from that, the Internationalists nevertheless questioned the need to be too slavishly tied to Stalin's apron strings.

There were other difficulties too. In the hurry to form

almost instant governments as nations were liberated by
the Red Army, there was not much time to examine the
record of each and every functionary who received an
appointment. Alongside those Communists who had been
in the struggle from the earliest days came men who had
joined the party the moment they realized that it would
emerge from the war victorious. There was a ready market
for careerists, adventurers and plain scoundrels.

In the early days the party could do little about them.
Equally, like it or not, it had to employ civil servants who
had served their right-wing predecessors or even the Germans during the occupation. Most of these accepted the
new diktats as readily as they accepted the old. These fledgling states had need of the experience and expertise of
these dubious people.

There were other problems of personnel. Among both
Muscovites and Internationalists there were genuine revolutionary heroes who had to be given senior posts but who
simply lacked the intelligence to do the job. At the same
time there were, in both factions, men who were playing a
double game. Several men given high government posts as
respected Communists had, in fact, been introduced into
the prewar illegal Communist parties as *agents provocateurs*. Others had become agents of the secret police after
arrest and perhaps torture. There were Muscovites who
had sold their souls long ago to Moscow and who were
full-paid agents of the Russian secret police. Equally,
among the Internationalists there were men who had—as
was suspected of them all—sold out to either the British or
the Americans.

The political posture increasingly being adopted by
Truman's America aggravated Stalin's often paranoiac suspicion of the West. In the immediate postwar years a large
immigrant population from Eastern Europe who were

vociferous in their prescriptions for the ills of their mother countries dominated the foreign policy of the State Department. Many of them had been distinguished prewar politicians, academics and journalists who had fled in the face of the advancing Red Army. Except for direct intelligence, these people provided American policy makers with the only evidence available of conditions in the satellites.

The result was an increasingly unreal diplomatic posture based upon increasingly unreal information. Though there were many disagreements among the refugees, on one matter they were united: their fellow countrymen in Poland, Hungary, Czechoslovakia, Yugoslavia, Bulgaria, Rumania, Albania and the Baltic States were merely waiting for the signal to overthrow their Communist masters. Held down by a vicious secret-police system, they needed only the right kind of encouragement to revolt. Western policy has still not thrown off this somewhat distorted view of the East European countries, and the tragedy of the Cold War years stemmed directly from it.

But in fact, the peoples of Eastern Europe welcomed the Red Army as liberators. Politically—whatever the old rightist refugee politicians in America believed to the contrary—the war had cauterized their politics; they were ready for socialism and a friendly, firm alliance with the Soviet Union. Most of their economists saw that while American aid would help rebuild their shattered industries, they had to turn eastward for trade. Their fate was inextricably bound by geography with the Soviet Union. If that meant adapting some of their political institutions to fit in with their new partner, then so be it.

Stalin, of course, felt justified in demanding rather more, and it was on that level that he could have been successfully challenged. Unfortunately, the West decided to fight him on the wrong ground. Instead of denouncing his

Russian imperialistic designs—dragging countries like Poland and Hungary kicking and screaming into the Soviet empire—America and her allies chose to talk of "Communist imperialism."

Thus did they totally undermine the position of nationalists who believed, rightly or wrongly, that the application of Marxist teachings in their countries was the way forward, but who, at the same time, were prepared to argue the Czech or the Polish or the Hungarian road to socialism. They wanted to be independent of Russia and America, though they saw that it was probably necessary to be interdependent with the Soviet Union.

A large proportion of the intelligentsia of their respective countries agreed with them and were prepared to face the consequences of the political battle of maintaining a position independent of the Soviet Union. And, in the early days, it looked as if they were winning.

But the American response made their position untenable. By equating communism with Russian imperialism, the Americans adopted a line similar to the Stalinist position: the satellites had to make a choice between Russia and America, between communism and capitalism. It was not possible to be a Hungarian Communist and accepted as such by Russia and America. Both sides decreed that one had to be a Communist or an anti-Communist. A Communist was someone who accepted "the leading role of the Soviet Union"; an anti-Communist was pro-American and anti-Russian.

While Andrei Vishinsky's claim that America was "attempting the economic enslavement of Europe through a policy of handouts" was monstrously unjust to a nation which was freely and willingly seeking to rebuild a battered Europe, there was already enough truth in this accusation to make it difficult for East European countries to accept the good offices of the United States without running the risk of seriously damaging their relations with the Soviet Union.

Two telegrams, one from U.S. Secretary of State James F. Byrnes to Ambassador Steinhardt and one from Steinhardt to Byrnes during the peace conference in Paris in October 1946, recently released by the State Department, bring this issue into focus.

The Americans had been complaining of the virulence of anti-U.S. propaganda in the Czech press and also the slowness with which Czechoslovakia, not then a Communist satellite, was responding to American requests for compensation after the recent nationalization of their property. In order to put pressure upon the Czech government the U.S. temporarily cut off all aid to Czechoslovakia. Steinhardt saw Prime Minister Gottwald, who agreed with him that the press had been unnecessarily brutal and also promised speedily to settle outstanding American claims. Steinhardt asked Byrnes, in light of this, to resume aid as a mark of American good faith.

Byrnes's reply from Paris was a remarkable one:

I am gratified to learn that the Czechoslovakian government is apparently beginning to realize that its policy of hostility towards the U.S., of ignoring our just claims and of persistent press attacks, may be productive of results as far as economic assistance is concerned which are not in the interests of Czechoslovakia. You must bear in mind, however, that up to the very end of this conference Czechoslovakia has consistently opposed the United States and voted unanimously with the Slav bloc on every important issue. We certainly could not expect any delegation to agree with us on all matters but when they disagree with us on every vote on every treaty, it confirms the unfriendly attitude hitherto expressed in the press. I should wish to see much more substantial evidence of Czechoslovakian independence and friendship towards the United States before resuming any form of economic assistance.

This telegram was the first to enunciate the principle that American aid depended upon a measure of political support. True, this was not yet enshrined as American policy, and the Marshall Plan retreated most honorably from it, but the course of future events was being set.

Steinhardt's reply was equally remarkable, containing, as it did, through the voice of Jan Masaryk, son of the founder of the Czechoslovakian Republic and a Democratic Non-Communist Socialist, a moving and eloquent testimony of the agony of Eastern Europe and a plea to the West to understand how the cause of freedom could best be served.

After an interview with Masaryk, Steinhardt reported back to Byrnes:

Under circumstances Masaryk deemed it preferable to vote with Soviet Union on almost every occasion that Poland and Yugoslavia had done so, convinced the United States was not harmed thereby, whereas Czechoslovakia might benefit. He pointed out that, as a result of Czechoslovakia's voting record, Soviets had scrupulously refrained from interfering in Czechoslovakia's internal affairs and that, in consequence, moderates were making steady progress in leading the country back to democratic ways. He argued that Czechoslovakia's return in the near future to its post-war standards of democracy made possible by non-interference by Soviets would in long run be of greater benefit to the United States than meaningless votes at international conferences. . . ."

It is difficult to fault Masaryk's line today.* Clearly, by 1946 two opposing pressures began to exert themselves upon what the Americans were beginning to call "the captive nations." The Soviets demanded political support in return for noninvolvement in internal affairs, and the Americans were already demanding at least some political support in exchange for aid. One does not need to be a logician to see that these two demands were incompatible and that Europe would be torn apart if there was an attempt to make them become so.

What American policy makers were unable to see was that communism as such did not have to be the bogey, that there was no reason at all why two economic systems, capitalism and communism, should not coexist. World Communist revolution was in any case outdated by the technological revolution which was changing so rapidly the lot of the traditionally underprivileged in all of the advanced nations; Marxism was retrogressive and old-fashioned; a country whose state religion was atheism was no more regrettable than a state founded—like Israel, which America was so busily supporting—solidly upon theocratic lines.

So the U.S. laid its long-term plans. Just as the old prewar Comintern had sponsored treason and sabotage in the West, seeking to undermine its institutions, the Americans would play the game in reverse. Apparently it did not occur to them that Russia had been remarkably, almost laughably, ineffective. Many believed, as the Senate Committee on Communist Aggression said in 1953, that " ... peaceful co-existence is a Communist myth which can be

---

* Jan Masaryk agreed to continue as foreign minister after the *Putsch*, but he died, tragically, on March 10, 1948, after falling from the window of his official apartment. Whether he jumped, slipped or was pushed has been the subject of continuous controversy ever since. Despite several investigations, official and unofficial, the incident has never been satisfactorily explained.

attained only through the complete surrender of our free way of life for one of slavery under Moscow-controlled Communism." The government lacked confidence in America's own way of life and its ability to withstand the patently inefficient and unhappy Communist experiment.

The muddled thinking which seemed to characterize this period was manifested in the security hysteria over the secret of the atomic bomb. Seen as the prime target for Soviet spies, America's atomic monopoly produced loyalty oaths, treason trials, congressional hearings—all of which inflamed anti-Communist passions within the country. Just as in wartime Britain people were asked to believe that "walls have ears," so in America the belief that there was a Communist spy around every corner was quite deliberately sown by politicians and the right-wing press. Few people saw the danger. Henry Stimson, President Truman's Republican secretary of war, urged America to share openly her atomic secrets with Russia in order to ward off a "secret armament race of a rather desperate character," but this idea, however far-seeing, was never given serious consideration. Instead, the U.S. built up an internal security apparatus, tougher and more ruthless than anything it had had during the war. Together with that came a propaganda campaign launched against Communists and Communist sympathizers, using the worldwide anxiety which the bomb engendered to instill in the American people and America's allies the belief that they were safe only as long as Russia did not have the atomic bomb.

Now, of course, it is possible to look back and see how unnecessary all of this was—not so much because events have weakened the political argument but because the intelligence agencies were mistaken in their one area of expertise: security. As Norbert Wiener has said in *The Human Use of Human Beings*, "When we consider a problem of nature such as atomic reaction and atomic explosion, the largest single item of information which we can make public is that they exist. Once a scientist attacks a problem which he knows to have an answer, his attitude is changed. He is already some fifty per cent of his way towards that answer."

The American government itself had given away the secret of the A-bomb when, on August 6, 1945, an American stratocruiser dropped an atomic bomb on the city of Hiroshima. From that moment on, Russia's possession of such a weapon became inevitable; they would get the bomb, and quickly.

Spy mania was at its height on the other side of the Iron Curtain too. This was exaggerated by the presence in Eastern Europe, France and Germany of the agents from old wartime espionage networks who now sought new masters to serve. American embassies in all of the Eastern European countries were besieged by local nationals offering their services, usually in order to buy their passage to the United States. But more than that, operations were launched by former members of the Office of Strategic Services (OSS) inside Eastern Europe from centers in West Germany which, while they may have had military backing, had little political sophistication or maturity. They proved to be totally nonproductive and indeed counterproductive. Every time Eastern Europe's secret police found a genuine spy or evidence of a parachute drop into their territory, they merely tightened security and suppressed their peoples still further.

It was in fact one of the ironies of the period that though the Russians imagined there was an American agent behind every bush, there were actually very few, and those who did exist were by and large incompetent not only in training but in the technology of espionage. At the end of the war President Truman disbanded the OSS on the theory that there was no need in time of peace to waste money upon an intelligence agency. It was an admirable point of view, harking back to that great period of American naïveté after World War I when Henry Stimson disbanded the decoding department of the State Department with the words "Gentlemen don't read other people's mail." So America entered the Cold War totally unprepared to fight it. A few attachés working for military intelligence, a few people attached to the State Department's own intelligence operation and a few OSS men attached to military missions in Europe were all there was on the ground. The quality of information which was brought in was, on the whole, of an extremely low grade.

Truman soon realized that he had been somewhat impetuous, but he was still apparently not convinced of the need for a full-scale peacetime OSS-style operation until 1947, when the Central Intelligence Agency was established by the National Security Act and headed by Rear Admiral Roscoe Hillenkoeter.

But even then the CIA was only given the task of "coordinating" the role of America's other unimpressive intelligence agencies. It was not really until the summer of 1948 that the National Security Council, under NSC 10/2, gave the CIA the authority "to carry through clandestine operations which the NSC directed." It would of course be wrong to suggest that clandestine operations had not been carried out before. The CIA Soviet desk, for example, under Polish-born Lieutenant Commander Samuel Frankel and Marine Colonel Harold Morie, who both had got into the business through their experience as American naval attachés in Murmansk during the war, was a virtually autonomous unit, running operations with verve, flair and imagination.

Equally, the CIA had already taken over the remarkable Russian anti-Soviet network of General Reinhardt Gehlen, who had offered to serve the Americans at the end of the war as faithfully as he had served Hitler. Though there was an initial reluctance among some quarters to use what was regarded as the tainted information of a tainted man, this view soon disappeared as the reality of the Cold War bore in on American policy makers.

Meanwhile, as each side was building up its intelligence agencies from which would come the front-line troops of the Cold War, relations between East and West deteriorated to the point where they ceased to exist. The possibility of a nuclear war was always on the horizon. Each camp rearmed feverishly and, in order to explain why that was necessary to their citizenry, stepped up the propaganda to a level of desperate intolerance. Diplomacy degenerated to plain abuse. Understanding and reason were expelled from the political dictionary. The anti-Communist witch-hunt created a wave of hysteria in America; the secret police moved through Russia and Eastern Europe like locusts, destroying all before them.

The times were ripe for every kind of excess. This is the story of one of them. It is the story of an intelligence operation; it is also, in a small way, the story of our times.

Chapter 1
The Park-Bench Rendezvous

The sharp winds picked up the dust of war, giving new life to what had been inanimate rubble. The atmosphere was full of the flecks of dirt which had become, in recent years, as much a part of Warsaw as was the Vistula River. An occasional tram clattered by with a shower of sparks, illuminating those shell-shocked ruins, grandiloquent testimonies all to the unsparing efficiency of the *Wehrmacht*. The winter sky provided a gloomy blanket for an already gloom-wracked city. An occasional civilian, huddled into himself against the cold, scurried past; a platoon of Soviet troops stumbled by, their boots dirty, their uniforms shabby and their spirit crushed by the hatred surrounding them as they went about their daily business. It was hard for them to understand: hadn't they, after all, liberated Poland from the Nazis, the common enemy which had so wantonly destroyed this once-beautiful city?

Their political officer had tried to explain it to them. The reactionaries still had not loosened their age-old hold over the Polish people. The enemy and its agencies, like the church, were everywhere, and until they were rooted out, their poisonous campaign against the Red Army and its glorious leader, Joseph Stalin, would continue unabated. But still the troops were puzzled—victory should not have been like this.

Captain Michael Sullivan stood in the doorway of what once had been a department store and was now a crumbling façade with nothing but yawning emptiness behind it, and watched them pass. There was no need for him to hide, for his documents were in order and his reasons for being in a part of town which few foreigners visited on anything but well-organized tours of inspection would stand up to any scrutiny. Still, he reasoned, there was no purpose in showing himself unnecessarily.

Recently his nerves had been stretched to breaking point and, if challenged now, he was no longer sure whether he could keep the anxiety out of his voice. The chances that the Soviets were setting a trap seemed disproportionately great—even London, who urged him to the *Treff*,* accepted that. Yet the possibility that the Pole really wanted to defect was so fascinating a prospect that London decreed that whatever the risk the approach had to be made.

Every precaution had been taken to mitigate potential disaster. Sullivan, head of the Secret Intelligence Service (SIS) operation in Poland, had been totally isolated from both his network and its reorganization. A new resident† had been flown in to take over as soon as Sullivan was brought out into the open. The most useful agents had

* An espionage term for a clandestine meeting.
† In intelligence jargon, the resident is the senior espionage agent of a network in a foreign country.

been moved out of the country in case Sullivan was picked up and forced under torture to name them. For the same reason, the new resident's identity was kept secret from Sullivan.

The elaborate communications network which he had built up since 1945 had been completely dismantled and a new system was being established. Sullivan's contacts in neighboring countries, both British and domestic, were warned and some were reposted. His Majesty's Secret Intelligence Service did not like to leave things to chance. For if Sullivan was walking into a trap, then so thorough were the preparations that the information he could provide the opposition would be of only historic value. There were, of course, immense dangers in what was being done. Bringing in new men in a hurry increases immeasurably the chances of introducing double agents. Indeed, there were some in London who opposed Sullivan making the meeting because they feared a subtle Russian plot to force SIS to dismember its efficient organization in Poland so that the Russians in turn could log in each newcomer as he came in and introduce men of their own. This view was rejected because, as Sir Stuart Menzies, head of SIS in Britain, liked to say, once you grant the enemy a mind so supreme that it thinks of everything, you are left with no choice but to do nothing.

Even the knowledge that the British had "boxed in" an active MGB* agent whom they would pick up and exchange for him if things went wrong didn't help Sullivan's peace of mind. He had worked long enough in Eastern Europe to know how much interrogators could do to a man in just a few short days.

One of the most important links in an espionage net-

---

* The MGB, the Ministry of State Security, was responsible for Soviet espionage overseas. In 1954 the MGB gave way to the now famous KGB, the Committee of State Security.

work is the legal, a kind of spy-ambassador in the country
to which he is accredited. While he knows nothing of his
nation's espionage activities in that country, he can contact his senior resident within hours. His function is to
effect exchanges, to receive warnings from the host country
about the activities of his resident and generally to help
undo the cumbersome tangles which any espionage service
leaves in its wake. The other side knows him for what he is,
but on his own side only his ambassador—and not always
he—is permitted to know his real function. In view of the
legal's presence, His Excellency never needs to dip so much
as a toe into the murkier waters of diplomacy.

Sullivan had been brought into this business when,
only three weeks earlier, the Pole had contacted the British legal through a go-between, indicating that he wished
to make certain arrangements with the British. The legal
then passed the message on to Sullivan along with the
man's credentials. Immediately the Pole was given a cover
name, Alice. Alice made it plain that, if the British were
interested, he would meet with no one but the resident
himself, and that such a meeting was to take place within
three weeks at a prearranged spot. It didn't take London
long to decide that Sullivan should make the meeting. If
anything went wrong, he now thought bitterly, he faced,
at best, a few uncomfortable days, and at worst, a bullet
in the back of the neck.

In many ways Sullivan—though that was almost certainly not his real name—was typical of his breed. His education had been conventional: a minor public school, Cambridge University, the army and eventually the wartime
Special Operations Executive (SOE). His transfer from
SOE to SIS came about because of one qualification: he
spoke fluent Polish. His father, a paper manufacturer
whose business had been almost exclusively with the Poles,

learned Polish himself and insisted that the language be spoken at home. As a result, Sullivan got a degree in Eastern European languages and a job with SOE. But SIS had more important plans for him. From the early forties it saw that the defeat of Germany would lead to perhaps a greater war with Russia over Poland, so Sullivan was kept away from the Poles so he would not be compromised in any way.

As soon as Poland was liberated, Sullivan went there as head of a British relief agency and, using charity as his cover, set up one of the most complex and sophisticated political intelligence networks then operating anywhere in the world. His network became the hub of the huge anti-Communist, anti-Russian resistance movement. Prominent anti-Communists were lifted out to safety, occasionally from the inside of prisons; sabotage and terrorism were almost daily occurrences. He sparked off, for example, an enormous run on the shops by spreading stories of shortages; rural riots, by letting it be known that the farms of the peasants were to be collectivized; or angry sermons from the nation's pulpits, by suggesting that holy places were to be desecrated. Remnants of the anti-Communist Home Army, who had fought so bravely against the Germans, were encouraged not to lay down their arms but to bide their time for the counterrevolution. In 1945, on instructions from headquarters, Sullivan and his agents had helped incite intense anti-Semitic demonstrations in Kielce and Krakow.

In the early days there were occasions when success —a countrywide explosion leading to the overthrow of the government—seemed close at hand. But this was 1948 and Sullivan knew that that battle had been lost. In Poland the secret police, the Urzad Bezpieczenstwa (known to every citizen as the UB or Bezpieka), had at last managed to gain control, and once they got it, with the help of their Soviet advisers, they were unlikely to let go easily. Where once Sullivan's men, nearly all of whom were Polish citizens, had appeared to have immunity as they moved up and down the country causing disruption and havoc, now they were being picked up on an almost daily basis. A *Putsch* had brought the Communists to total power in Czechoslovakia, and in Hungary, Rumania, Bulgaria and Albania, the methods of Stalin and the whole of the Stalinist terror machine were in force. What had once been fertile territory for the kind of campaign Sullivan was running had now become barren soil as the population, taught to believe that all their troubles were the result of the West's war preparations, became more and more frightened and hostile.

Though Sullivan never for a moment doubted the rightness of his cause, he did tend now to question its usefulness. He was tired. Every action was that much more difficult to plan. Many of his best people had been arrested. He no longer had the organization, the manpower or the contacts on the inside. And now, as if to underline his changing status, he was being brought out into the open to meet the man who was one of his principal adversaries.

Sullivan walked slowly to his destination. There had been yet another power cut, so none of the streetlamps were working. He stumbled on pieces of brick and fallen masonry and soon reached a bench by the old fortifications where the meeting was to take place. He looked at his watch: five minutes to go before the *Treff*. He had arrived early—an act of indiscipline which would be impossible today, for the clock is an agent's first line of defense against a blown cover. You either arrive on time or you don't arrive at all—it's as simple as that.

Sullivan took his seat and looked around fearfully.

Only the greatest effort of will stopped him from getting to his feet and running to the comfort of his room at the Hotel Polonia. Then he saw Alice, alone, rounding the wall carefully, as he had done, picking his way between the stones. He was astonished to see how young the Pole was and for a moment thought that perhaps this was not his man after all. But then he remembered that Alice would be but thirty-two years old.

The man motioned to Sullivan to remain seated. He was dressed in a rather shabby blue suit, with a too-long raincoat open in front as if defying the cold. He smiled briefly and sat down beside the British agent.

"I'm here," Sullivan said a little inanely. "You have a proposal?"

Alice nodded. His name was Jozef Swiatlo. Though his face was totally unknown as yet, he was one of the twelve most influential and feared men in Poland.

Yes, he had a proposal: Lieutenant Colonel Jozef Swiatlo wished to defect.

Chapter 2
The Polish Nightmare

Lieutenant Colonel Jozef Swiatlo, young though he was, personified all that it was to be a helpless victim of Polish history. Like so many, he suffered terrible dilemmas of conscience and national pride. He was a part of that fierce political whirlpool which turned Pole against Pole and eventually sucked the country down into the quagmire of the Cold War. It had never been easy to be a Pole, and in 1948 Russia and America, between them, made it all but impossible.

Jozef Swiatlo came from a poverty-stricken home in a society which appeared, in his eyes, to thrive on social injustice. Clever and ambitious, angered by what he described subsequently as "the terrible economic conditions in which I and my family were living," he left school at the age of sixteen, joined the outlawed Communist party when he was eighteen and soon made his mark as an outstanding new recruit in the local party cell.

During Swiatlo's childhood, his homeland was struggling to preserve its autonomy. From the West, new, militant Fascist Germany was determined to wrest from Poland what it had lost at Versailles after the First World War. In the East, Stalin thought of Poland not only as Russia's traditional enemy but as the central chain of the hated *cordon sanitaire* which the Western powers had established on the borders of the Soviet Union in order to prevent the virus of communism from contaminating their own citizenry. Poland's ineffectual "government of the colonels" sought vainly to balance these opposing forces. Without actually ever being pro-Russian, they also took care not to be pro-German in either their domestic or foreign policies. For an illegal underground party such as the Communists, this lack of any clear-cut philosophy to oppose made their task of rallying opinion against the government that much more frustrating. Polish Communists like the young Swiatlo faced another dilemma too: Polish nationalism demanded that the Eastern boundaries, won from Russia in a war between the two countries in 1920, should remain inviolate. The Kremlin thought otherwise.

Most solved this predicament by embracing the beliefs of that great Polish Communist Rosa Luxemburg, killed in Germany in 1919, who called for a truly international Socialist society in which there would be no place for an independent Poland *or* Russia. To Stalin it sounded like outright heresy—Trotskyism at its very worst. In 1938, angered by the misconduct of Polish Communists and motivated by his ideas on how Germany and Russia could carve up Poland, Stalin expelled the entire Polish Commu-

nist party from the Communist International, the Comintern. Most Polish Communists in Moscow at the time were
either executed or deported to prison camps.

Back home, party members either drifted away or, like
Swiatlo, who was arrested twice, were imprisoned. The
movement Swiatlo had joined as a young man was finally
shattered when, after the outbreak of war on September 1,
1939, as the German army launched its *Blitzkrieg* against
Poland, Russia cynically exploited the situation and
exercised her rights under the Molotov-Ribbentropp pact
to seize the Eastern half of Poland and share a now battered country with the Germans.

In June 1941, when Swiatlo was twenty-six years old,
the rules changed once again. Hitler invaded the Soviet
Union, in Operation Barbarossa, and suddenly Poland
found herself an ally with the Russians in the common
struggle against the Nazis. Russia established diplomatic
relations with the Polish government-in-exile in London,
and it was agreed that the Soviet-German Treaty of 1939,
which divided Poland between the two conquering powers,
had lost its validity.

The Poles deported by the Russians as the Soviet
Union took possession of its half of the country were
released by the thousands and permitted to form a Polish
army under General Wladyslaw Anders and make their
way out of Russia via Persia to fight under British command. Swiatlo, who in 1938 had been drafted into the army
and become a German prisoner of war, managed to escape
from his camp, and he and other Poles formed an army
under General Sigmund Berling to fight on the Russian
front. For a short time Poland and Russia seemed to be
fighting the same war against the same enemy. But it
couldn't last. Stalin soon made it clear that once Germany
had been defeated he proposed to secure his frontiers by

moving eastward into Poland and establishing the Soviet-Polish border along the Curzon Line of 1920.

On January 4, 1944, when the Red Army crossed the prewar Polish frontier and liberated from the Germans the first few kilometers of Polish soil, Pole was set inalterably against Pole. But the politicians saw it differently: Polish territory might be free, but the heart of Poland was still not spoken for. A few days later leading Polish Communists, together with a few left-wing sympathizers, knowing that it would be the Red Army and not the British or the Americans who would eventually set the country free, set up a National Council to administer all of the newly liberated territories. This act drove the London government, backed as it was by the Home Army, to announce the formation of a Council of National Unity designed to hold the fort until the London government could return and resume its rightful place at the head of the Polish State.

Stalin's line was simple: he would accept any anti-Fascist Polish government which recognized the validity of the Curzon Line. Churchill pleaded with the London Poles to accept the Curzon Line so that they could return to help form a new, broadly based government. But they were obdurate: the borders of Poland must be inviolate. Unable to gain support anywhere, the Polish government-in-exile soon lapsed into a state of impotence.

Meanwhile, the Red Army swept through Poland. In July 1944, while Swiatlo was holding down the key job of a political officer in the Berling army, it crossed the Curzon Line and immediately set up, in the town of Lublin, the Polish Committee of National Liberation—henceforth known as the Lublin Committee. It soon became apparent that the Soviets proposed to recognize this body, rather than the government in London, as the nucleus of the future government of Poland. Stalin demanded an administration which could guarantee his soldiers fighting a ruthless enemy in front that they did not also have to spend their time protecting their rear against a hostile local guerrilla army.

These fearful political differences came to a head at five o'clock in the afternoon of August 1, 1944, when the people of Warsaw arose as one against the Nazi invader. General Bor Komorowski, national commander of the Home Army in Warsaw, had enough food and ammunition to wage modern urban warfare for seven days. In the first fantastic forty-eight hours his army of 40,000 captured two thirds of the city from the Germans. Victory seemed theirs, for just across the Vistula stood the Red Army, poised for its final assault upon the city, with all the armor necessary to crush the German counterattack. For two months the battle raged. The Red troops, within hailing distance of the city, sat by their silent guns and waited. Eventually the Germans regained the upper hand. Life was slowly and inexorably squeezed out of Warsaw as the Germans, block by block, laid waste to the city as a punishment for what had been without doubt the most glorious moment of national resistance during the entire war. But it had all been for nothing.

For one thing went wrong: Marshal Stalin simply looked the other way. So Warsaw bled to death: two hundred thousand Poles lost their lives, and with them perished the last hopes of the government-in-exile in London. By the time the Red Army stirred itself, the city was a physical, moral and political desert. A vacuum had been created, and the Lublin Committee and the NKVD*

---

* The People's Commissariat for Internal Affairs. It shared with the NKGB, the People's Commissariat for State Security, the function of secret police for the Soviet Union. In 1946 the "commissariats" became "ministries," and so the NKVD became the MVD and the NKGB the MGB.

were ready to fill it. The nation was in the hands of its
Jozef Swiatlos.

Patriotism can take many forms. Swiatlo chose a
course which Poles outside Poland, anywhere in the world,
find difficult to understand. As a political officer in the Berling army, he realized that any rational political argument
was out of place in the atmosphere created by the war.
Moreover, he, and Communists like him, saw that the lack
of objectivity being displayed by their legal government in
London was leading Stalin to distrust Poland. Their best
hope, then, was to establish in Warsaw a government
friendly enough to Stalin to assuage his grave suspicions,
and at the same time independent enough to satisfy their
own patriotic fervor. The tragedy is that they lost that
battle, just as the London government had previously lost
its battle.

Swiatlo and his friends acted with total ruthlessness in
1944 and 1945 as the Kosciuszko Division of the Berling
army swept through Poland, rounding up elements they
regarded as hostile to the Red Army, setting an example
for Stalinist terror tactics which were subsequently copied
with even greater effect in other satellites.

Polish Communists were faced with a subtly difficult
choice. The feeling in Poland, especially among the adher-
ents of the London government, was that any who cooperated with the Soviets were traitors to their country. Yet as
the London Poles hardened their policies against the Russians, they were forced to intensify the outward expression
of their commitment to a Poland allied politically, diplomatically and militarily with the Soviet Union in order to
convince Stalin that Poland could and should rule itself.

As the Home Army turned its guns upon the "libera-
tor," the Polish Communist secret police was forced to act
with increasing toughness in order to persuade the NKVD
that this was a Polish problem which could be dealt with

by Poles and that Russian intervention was unnecessary.

The majority of Poles were so anti-Communist, so anti-Russian and so brutalized by a fearful war that without the presence of the Red Army the country would have been lost within twenty-four hours and a government totally hostile to Stalin established within seven days. So he demanded more in the way of tribute. Soon men like Swiatlo had completely pinned their colors to Stalin's masthead.

Once Russian power over Poland had become a reality, further concessions were made in order to satisfy the Russians that Poland could rule herself within the Soviet bloc. But, by this time, the Cold War was gathering momentum. The fight had become one between superpowers; Poland no longer mattered. Russia required from her only military divisions and the right kind of subservience to assure loyalty.

The Soviets were in command, and those who did not accept this reality were soon shown the error of their ways by a secret-police apparatus, one of the commanders of which was Jozef Swiatlo. The Bezpieka, or UB, like the secret police of any totalitarian government, soon became the only organization inside Poland which mattered. Everything was subordinated to its needs. Only President Boleslaw Bierut was privy to all of its secrets, and even he knew that at any time the UB could be used against himself.

By 1948, the year Swiatlo approached SIS with his offer to defect, it consisted of nineteen departments and employed a personnel of thousands. Officers of the UB were the new aristocracy. Rank-and-filers received salaries four or five times higher than the average skilled industrial workers; they were given priority in housing and permitted to purchase luxury goods in special shops to which the general public was not admitted. With food desperately short, UB canteens in Warsaw presented lavish dishes not seen in Poland since before the war. It was a privileged existence above the law, and few, once inside, were prepared to risk sacrificing their jobs by a display of scruple which could antagonize their Soviet masters. For the UB was under the direct control of the Kremlin-appointed MVD* officers on local secondment, sharing the top positions with Polish colleagues.

The first department was engaged in counterespionage against the activities of foreign intelligence services. The second department dealt with archives, censored mail from abroad and newspapers, and was headed directly by a Soviet colonel. The third, fourth and fifth departments, each under the tandem leadership of a Polish and a Russian colonel, dealt with internal subversive organizations, espionage and sabotage in light industry, and subversion in the non-Communist political parties. The sixth, eighth and ninth departments dealt with administration of the labor camps and prisons in Poland, heavy transport, and sabotage in heavy industry. The seventh department dealt with espionage abroad and the eleventh department with the Catholic church, which was always regarded as potentially hostile.

The most important department, the tenth, came directly under the head of the Russian secret police, Lavrenti Beria. Department 10 had as its chief the sinister and ruthless Colonel Anatol Fejgin, but orders usually came from the most powerful man at the top of the party apparatus, Jakub Berman.

Department 10 was responsible for the ideological and political purity of the Polish Communist party and govern-

* The Ministry of the Interior, responsible at that time for counterespionage in the USSR and in the satellites.

ment. Its function was to police the policemen of this
police state. It maintained files on every party member in
the nation as well as the neighboring countries of the Communist bloc, looking for incriminating evidence against its
own leaders. It had the power to interrogate subordinates
about their ministers and to order ministers to dismiss
their subordinates. Every peccadillo, every rumor, every
example of disloyalty to either President Bierut or Moscow
was filed away for future reference. As the files on the
party members grew thicker, so grew the power of the
members of Department 10.

These files, not necessarily nor even most often
required for immediate use, were Stalin's insurance policy
against future misconduct. What better assurance of total
loyalty than if the party member concerned knew that one
step back and the incident with that little girl twenty
years before would suddenly be "discovered" and the dossier presented to the public prosecutor? What better assurance of total loyalty than the knowledge that the minister
in charge of public security had perhaps been an *agent
provocateur*?

Stalin's weapon inside Poland was Department 10 of
the Bezpieka. It was a feared and fearful organization, and
its deputy director was Jozef Swiatlo. By 1948, when this
story opened, Swiatlo had the Communist party and the
government of Poland in his hands. No secret was kept
from him. He could make or break a minister with the snap
of a finger. He was as important as that. ·

Chapter 3
The British Opt Out

The communications clerk in the sophisticated signals section of the Foreign Office in London switched the telex machine through to 21, Queen Anne's Gate, the headquarters of the SIS, and then watched the Foreign Office copy, on its pink paper, unfold its long sequences of coded gibberish before he tore off the paper and sent it by special messenger upstairs.

Almost at once the Sullivan report became the subject of virulent debate. Because of an extraordinary bureaucratic muddle, what should have been a British triumph became a disastrous mistake: in effect, SIS abdicated to the CIA its role as the Western world's most powerful intelligence apparatus.

Since the spy has taken over from the private eye as

our most popular postwar fictional hero, most of us have an unbalanced and faintly ridiculous image of what modern espionage is all about. Attention has focused, naturally enough, upon the man of action, but in intelligence terms, the operative is no more than a private in a privileged army of officers. Control is what counts, and that depends absolutely upon the evaluators. A report that a Communist functionary is on the way out is meaningless until the evaluators can show that the man represented a particular line of policy which will be jettisoned with him. A report of new military installations on the Arctic Circle means nothing until the evaluators produce a coherent picture of a new Soviet ICBM. Information makes the evaluators' task possible, but with poor evaluation 90 percent of all intelligence is worthless.

So it was to the evaluators that the Sullivan report first went. Their problem was to decide why Swiatlo wanted to defect; what benefits would accrue to Britain or the Western alliance if he did; and whether there was any risk that Swiatlo was part of a complex game of deception.

The reasons why a man decides to go to the other side usually provide the clue to his ultimate usefulness. Few men defect while they are at their peak. Indeed, most do so when they are so far on the outside that any information they can bring with them is of only historical value. Most defectors realize they are on the slide long after this has become evident to their colleagues, and SIS—unlike the CIA—has always exercised extreme caution in avoiding what it describes as "shop-worn goods."

It was clear from the outset that Swiatlo was far from shop-worn. Sullivan's report proved that Swiatlo was completely trusted by the Russians and respected by the Poles. He was incredibly young for the importance of his job, and

his future looked bright indeed. Equally, the quality of the
material in his possession was not only explosive but
totally up-to-date. He had access to the most secret
archives; he was trusted by the leadership and he had
everything to gain by staying. This fact, by itself, introduced a note of caution in some of the evaluators' reports:
Swiatlo had been too easy, almost too good to be true.

So possibly Swiatlo was being set up by the Russians.
Perhaps the MGB had devised a new way of infiltrating a
spy into the West by giving him a defector's cover, or, more
probably, decided to use Swiatlo to plant inaccurate information within Western intelligence during his debriefing.
If this was the case, then clearly it was an operation which
had been planned for years. If Swiatlo really was who he
said he was, then, under intensive debriefing, he could not
help but reveal facts which the Russians would not want
him to reveal. The only way such an operation could really
work would have been for Swiatlo, almost from the end of
the war, to have been given a phony job, in a phony
department, fed every day with phony data. He would
have had to have lived the part for years. On the face of it,
this seemed unlikely. Although the skill required to mount
such an operation existed then, it had not yet been put to
the kind of use which made an operation of this kind feas-
ible in later years.

So, Swiatlo was a genuine defector, but why? The reasons he gave Sullivan were classic: he had become a Communist out of honest conviction, but slowly and gradually
the realization of what communism was all about, the way
it brutalized the human spirit, first shocked and finally
sickened him. Disillusionment had given way to despair,
and now his only wish was to come to the West and fight
for the cause of freedom. He knew how his country had

become nothing more than a slave state of the Soviet Union and how its leaders were puppets in the hands of their Russian masters. This explanation was given credibility because Swiatlo was a highly successful young man with apparently more to lose than to gain by leaving his position of power and responsibility and coming to face an uncertain future in the West.

But Sullivan's theory, based upon carefully gleaned Warsaw information, was a little more subtle. Swiatlo, he said, had decided to come over almost on the spur of the moment, at the point where he lost a major battle with one of the most prominent personalities of the regime, Jakub Berman. A United Press stringer in Warsaw before the war while all the time a member of the Central Committee of the Polish Communist party, Berman became responsible for recruiting members of the intelligentsia into the party. After the war he became responsible for security and party ideology, and, thanks to his close friendship with Bierut, second only to the president in importance within the nation. It remains a mystery how Berman managed to remain unscathed before the war, especially when there was evidence from other Communists who had been arrested that the police knew about him. But to Swiatlo, who took an instant dislike to him, there was only one explanation: Berman had been in the pay of the postwar political police, who perhaps had even infiltrated him into the party as an *agent provocateur*.

There was no proof that Berman had cooperated in any way with the prewar police, but Swiatlo, convinced of his guilt, collected a dossier containing, at best, hearsay evidence and went straight to the president demanding a full-scale party investigation. Swiatlo was an ambitious man. With Berman out of the way, his own path to the top would be that much clearer, but that was not all that motivated him. Swiatlo took his job seriously. He knew well that, because of the checkered history of Poland during the past few years, not everyone was who he seemed to be; as the kaleidoscope was shaken up, villains emerged as heroes, Fascists became Communists and police spies became government ministers. It was the function of his department to find a pathway through this morass.

Instead of demanding some form of inquiry into Swiatlo's damning indictment, President Bierut ordered the arrest of one of Swiatlo's principal informants and then counseled Swiatlo to keep the whole affair to himself. At the same time Bierut did not discourage him from pursuing his inquiries into all of Berman's activities, past and present, but made it clear that these would be for "file purposes" only and that no action was contemplated or likely against his principal lieutenant. Disgusted by the way his report had been treated, Swiatlo decided to defect, the act of an angry man, frustrated by thwarted ambition and the belief that the system he had fought for all his life was corrupted beyond repair.

Captain Sullivan's report went on to argue that Swiatlo, having decided to defect in a moment of pique, could just as quickly change his mind. Speed was imperative, for if Swiatlo did regret what he had done, Sullivan's life would be worth no more than a bent zloty. Nothing, he emphasized, was on paper. Any subsequent attempt to persuade Swiatlo by blackmail to carry through with his plan could be easily brushed aside as an SIS provocation. But then he, Sullivan, would have to be removed, and that was, for the evaluators, enough to make them ignore his theory. No man who betrays the fact that he may have lost his nerve is permitted his own evaluations. Another explanation had to be found. Swiatlo had made a few innocuous remarks to Sullivan about the high standard of living in the West, so for lack of a better motive SIS assumed that the Pole's interests were "material." Simply because "material" defections from East to West were the most common, SIS tended to give them a grade-two classification, but in Swiatlo's case this proved to be a catastrophic mistake. The most important defector who had come the way of the British since the war was almost lost for good.

A grade-two defector is granted permission to come to Britain and stay but is given minimal assistance in making the journey or setting himself up once he arrives. During the late forties, there were hundreds of minor officials, usually non-Communist, from all over Eastern Europe, who were in trouble because of some past connection with Britain. Once processed by the British embassies in their respective countries, the requests for asylum went to the home secretary for signature. But this time he balked. There were too many such defectors; there was little they could do for Britain, and Britain, who in only a few cases had any moral duty, could do little for them. He sent the list to Foreign Secretary Ernest Bevin, the nominal ministerial head of SIS. If there were overriding reasons of foreign policy why these requests should be granted, then the orders would be signed, but not otherwise. The practice was no longer to be an automatic one.

To the total surprise of SIS, Bevin now dug his heels in firmly. He scornfully attacked British intelligence methods inside Eastern Europe as embarrassingly worse than useless. The satellites were a lost cause, he said; political intelligence in capitals like Warsaw, Budapest and Bucharest was a waste of time. SIS should concentrate its resources upon the fringe nations, countries where Britain still had an influence and where the threat of Communist takeover existed but was not yet a reality.*

Meanwhile, SIS realized with horror that the name of Jozef Swiatlo had been mixed up with much smaller fish. Permission to grant him political asylum had been refused with all the others, and with Bevin in his present mood, there was no way of altering that situation. In fact, Swiatlo was an invaluable find—an intelligence man's dream. And a quite incredible piece of incompetence almost lost him forever. Only those who have worked in a government department will know how such things are possible.

The SIS concern was now Captain Michael Sullivan. If Sullivan had to tell Swiatlo that nothing could be done for him, it was possible that, in order to protect himself, Swiat-

---

* Bevin's criticisms were largely unjust. Britain still operated the only really effective intelligence apparatus in the Western world. The Gehlen organization in West Germany was not yet operational. The French had too many internal problems to bother about espionage. As for the Americans, the debate was still raging in Washington as to whether a peacetime clandestine intelligence operation was necessary. This debate masked the reality of what was going on. The armed forces, the State Department and various private foundations were financing and stage-managing full-blooded operations, not only inside Eastern Europe but in the Soviet Union as well. This secret and not particularly professional army necessarily came off second best when pitted against the magnificently financed, equipped and trained MVD and the MGB, which emerged from the war stronger and more effective than ever before.

Bevin was instrumental in changing all of that. By withdrawing SIS from Eastern Europe, he weakened his organization immeasurably: it lacked the expertise to operate overnight as efficiently elsewhere and it began to spread its tentacles over too wide an area with too limited a budget. Into this vacuum in Eastern Europe stepped the professional anti-Communists of American and German intelligence. Murder and mayhem became increasingly common as the more sophisticated and traditional methods of SIS gave way to those of the newcomers. Possibly Bevin regarded SIS as being a kid-glove operation when more direct methods were called for. Perhaps he saw this as an opportunity to suck the Americans into a deeper and closer involvement with the affairs of Europe by making it impossible for them to rely any longer upon the one secret service whose information and expertise they could trust, and force them to set up their own apparatus.

lo would not only have Sullivan killed, but perhaps even strike at any remaining members of the Sullivan network. If it valued Sullivan, SIS could not risk removing him from the country in a hurry. The chances were that Swiatlo was having him watched during the seven days he had given SIS to come up with an answer. Any sudden move by Sullivan and that would probably be the end of him. It didn't take long to come up with the answer: an unofficial approach would be made to the Americans to ask them to take over from where Sullivan had left off.

Sullivan would be instructed to tell Swiatlo that the Americans were handling the case. With the disdain for American intelligence which SIS had at that time, it was hoped that the hob-nailed boots of American intelligence men tramping over the Polish landscape would persuade Swiatlo that the Americans were indeed in on the act, that the British had done their bit and that he would be well looked after. Sullivan had a further meeting with Alice, who accepted the decision and disappeared once again.*

Meanwhile, SIS sent a message to the British embassy in Washington, asking for an "unofficial" approach to be made to the Americans concerning Swiatlo. To the chief SIS man in Washington, the word "unofficial" meant only one thing. He picked up the telephone, called a number in New York and then boarded a train to keep the appointment he had just made with a senior partner in the famous old Wall Street law firm of Sullivan & Cromwell.

---

* Sullivan returned to London and subsequently worked in the Middle East. He died of a heart attack in Beirut in 1967.

Chapter 4

Over to the Man on Wall Street

Allen Welsh Dulles, son of a well-known Presbyterian minister, grandson of a secretary of state, a Phi Beta Kappa graduate of Princeton, a former Foreign Service officer and head of the OSS mission in Switzerland during World War II, had all it took to be accepted at the highest level anywhere on Wall Street. Pull he had in plenty. Tall, gregarious, soft-spoken, an intellectual gadfly dressed in slightly shabby tweeds in the manner of a man who doesn't need to keep up appearances, Dulles had contacts in the highest reaches of government. Although he was a senior partner of the distinguished Wall Street law firm of Sullivan & Cromwell, this was merely a cover and base of operations for his real activities, for despite a variety of jobs and interests, he never ceased to be what he became on leaving Princeton, a full-time member of the American intelligence establishment.

It was World War II which had catapulted him to the center of the international stage and given him the taste for high-level political adventure. (Eventually he was to become the bogeyman of leftists all over the world, but, like all stereotyped images, this view of him never really fitted.) William "Wild Bill" Donovan, head of the OSS, had recognized Dulles's genius for clandestine intelligence and placed him on the road to future greatness by giving him probably the most important station in his command, the OSS office in Berne, Switzerland—the natural crossroads of virtually all wartime intelligence. There Dulles quickly made his mark, but not as the obsessive anti-Communist he subsequently became. He saw the war as a fight against fascism, and he knowingly dealt with Communists because, as far as he was concerned, anyone who was prepared to help in that fight was good enough for him. Like most Americans of his class and education, he tended to regard Russia with admiration and communism as a harmless eccentricity, enjoyed by some of his friends. He considered the British Empire a greater threat to world peace than Russia; the first task after the war should be to dismember that empire and reduce Britain to a small offshore island of Europe. It is difficult now to remember how deep American intellectuals' antipathy was for the Empire, and while this may have been softened by the impact of Britain's heroic resistance to the Nazis, it still very much existed.

Russia, on the other hand, had a romantic appeal. The fantastic losses suffered by the Russian people, the holding of the Germans at the gates of Moscow and then the great victory of Stalingrad, unquestionably the turning point in the war, had captured the Americans' admiration. Stalin appeared to be an almost avuncular character to many,

and while the business community, right-wing members
of Congress and professional anti-Communists in the trade
union movement and elsewhere still feared the Bolshevik
menace, the political climate had changed sufficiently to
make this an unpopular attitude to express.

However, a particular experience helped change Allen
Dulles's mind: it was the occasion of a deep, personal dis-
appointment which, as he had exceeded instructions, could
have set his own career back considerably.*

On March 8, 1945, Major General Karl Wolff, a hard-
line Nazi and top SS man in Italy, met Allen Dulles in
Berne. Wolff, believing that a German surrender was vital
to stave off a Communist sweep across Europe, offered an
unconditional surrender of the one million German troops
in Italy and the probable surrender of the entire *Wehrmacht*. Immediately the negotiations were given the code
name "Sunrise," and, on the following day, staff officers
were on their way from Allied headquarters in Italy to
take part in the negotiations. On March 13 U.S. General
Lyman Lemnitzer and British General Terence Airey
arrived in Lyon for a meeting with Wolff, and on March 19
Wolff returned to Italy to sound out the *Wehrmacht* and
Berlin. Then, on April 20, Dulles, who believed he had carried off the greatest coup not only of his career but of any
intelligence man during World War II, received instructions from Washington to break off all contact.

What Dulles had forgotten, or perhaps deliberately
ignored, was the delicate stage of relations between

---

* Historians may feel that it is too glib an assumption to accept
that the public attitudes of a man like Dulles are likely to be shaped
by private disappointments. It is my view that this occurs more often
than not; personal affronts, shattered dignities and early frustrations
have a far greater effect upon the policies and beliefs of the leaders of
great nations than one really cares to admit. The need to believe that
our leaders lack human failings tends to obscure the very real effect
which these personal tragedies have upon them. Certainly most people
who knew Allen Dulles well agree that what occurred in Berne in 1945
had a profound impact upon him.

Moscow and Washington. When Stalin heard of the talks, he demanded Soviet participation. But since the purpose of Wolff's initiative was aimed at forestalling the Communists, British General Sir Harold Alexander, commander-in-chief in Italy, on the advice of Allen Dulles, rejected his request.

Stalin, in fact, knew what was going on from his own agents, who had been closely watching the progress of the talks. He believed the Germans had taken advantage of the talks to move three divisions from Italy to the eastern front and that, as he wrote in a letter to Roosevelt, General Kesselring, the German army commander in the West, had "agreed to open the front and permit the Anglo-American troops to advance to the east, and the Anglo-Americans [had] promised in return to ease the peace terms for the Germans."

Roosevelt replied angrily: "Frankly, I cannot avoid a feeling of bitter resentment towards your informers, whoever they are, for such vile misrepresentations of my actions or those of my trusted subordinates." Stalin answered: "I have never doubted your integrity or trustworthiness, just as I have never questioned the integrity or trustworthiness of Mr. Churchill." But the talks were called off, and the German armies in Italy did not surrender until six days before all the German forces in Europe surrendered. Before that happened, Dulles had to go through the personal indignity of rescuing General Wolff from Italian partisans who were surrounding his headquarters.

What was described by Roosevelt as "the Berne incident" has always slightly puzzled historians. Soviet-American relations had been good enough to assure Stalin that Roosevelt would not accept a surrender of German forces in Italy just so that they could be employed against the Red Army in the East, and certainly would not make a deal behind his back to allow the Anglo-American forces to sweep across Europe and hold the line against the onrushing Red Army. At the same time, the bitterness of Stalin's message was very real, and it cannot be assumed, as it has been by most historians, that Stalin, in a typically heavy-handed fashion, was making a political point or indulging his paranoia. He was deeply disturbed.

The fault lay with Allen Dulles. According to British sources, during the early stages of these negotiations he told Wolff what he thought the general wanted to hear. If Wolff could be persuaded to surrender the German army in Italy in exchange for promises as to America's future conduct toward the Red Army, then, as far as Dulles was concerned, that promise was worth making, even though there was no intention of delivering.*

At that stage of the war, his promises to Wolff, which

* Throughout the war in his negotiations with Nazis, Dulles had peppered his conversation with sentiments designed to persuade the Germans that if they followed the course of action he was proposing, the result would be to their advantage. Thus, in February 1943, in talks with Prince Maximilian Hohenlohe, an agent of Himmler's SS who was trying to persuade Dulles to sign a separate peace with the Third Reich, with Himmler as its *Führer*, Dulles told him, according to Hehenholle's report of the meeting, that he was "fed up with listening all the time to outdated politicians, *émigrés* and prejudiced Jews." Hehenholle reported that in Dulles's view, "a peace had to be made in Europe in the preservation of which all concerned would have a real interest. There must not again be a division into victor and vanquished that is contented and discontented: never again must nations like Germany be driven by want and injustice to desperate experiments and heroism. The German State must continue to exist as a factor of order and progress: there could be no question of its partition or the separation of Austria. . . . To the Czech question [Dulles] seemed to attach little importance. At the same time, he felt it necessary to support a *cordon sanitaire* against Bolshevism and Pan-Slavism through the eastward enlargement of Poland and the preservation of Rumania and a strong Hungary."

Left-wing critics of Allen Dulles have used this statement to support the contention that Dulles was a Fascist in everything but name. That, of course, is nonsensical. He fought the war with one aim in view —the defeat and dismemberment of Nazi Germany—but though his motives were always honorable, his methods, particularly in the Berne affair, were sometimes foolish. During these negotiations, Dulles went far beyond any possible brief he may have had in order to secure a hasty German surrender.

were relayed to Berlin, were foolhardy. Dulles should have
realized that so demoralized was Germany that the chances
of Soviet agents learning of these talks were better than
even, and this is what happened. When Stalin heard of the
Dulles offer, he took it at face value, especially as Dulles
had throughout the war somewhat exaggerated his influence upon Roosevelt. The net result was not the end of the
war in Italy but, just before Roosevelt's death, a major
confrontation between Russia and America. From that
moment on, the belief inside Stalin's Politburo that the
Western powers, having won the war against Germany,
would now turn upon their more traditional rival, Communist Russia, gained momentum, and the great wartime alliance began to fall apart at the seams.

It was a bitter and memorable moment for Dulles. He
felt Russian suspicion had prolonged the war and cost
needless lives in a theater where it was all but over. He
drew from the experience the lesson that Russia would do
anything to gain her postwar objectives, and he blamed
Roosevelt for sacrificing American lives in order to pacify
her cruel ambition. It was widely believed in British and
American circles that Dulles had mishandled the affair.
Interestingly, he subsequently claimed to have actually
secured the surrender of the German armies. Insofar as the
negotiations which he began eventually succeeded, since
Germany was on the point of capitulation, this was the
case. Insofar as gaining a meaningful *early* surrender was
concerned, he failed.

Unquestionably, all of this soured Dulles's relations
with "Wild Bill" Donovan who, after V-E Day, refused to
nominate Allen Dulles as OSS commander of the European
theater, a job to which, by seniority and experience, he was
entitled. Instead, he was appointed OSS director in the
American occupation zone in Germany and given a position of seniority well down the ladder.

By this time Dulles had become deeply anti-Communist and anti-Russian. The ruthless methods of the Red Army and the NKVD men who had arrived with them inside the Soviet zone of occupation and their total unwillingness to cooperate *on any level at all* hastened this process.

Seeing no future for himself in an intelligence operation rapidly being wound down, Allen Dulles left the OSS in 1946 and joined Sullivan & Cromwell. Apart from any other reason, he needed the money, and he was more likely to get it in a law firm than in government service. But he quickly discovered that after the excitement of his wartime job, the practice of law was a dull and pedestrian occupation. So when friends in the State Department suggested to him that there was room for him as a free-lance operator in the absence of a formal American intelligence operation, he leaped at the opportunity. He quickly established himself as one of the foremost intelligence men in the Western world.

From 1946 until 1948 Dulles ran private intelligence operations inside Eastern Europe with funds collected from wealthy friends and companies. Like his brother, John Foster, he was directly involved with a number of religious and charitable institutions, many with international connections and ramifications which offered a useful cover. Most of the operations concerned lifting distinguished anti-Communists out of Eastern Europe to freedom. Many of the escapes were unnecessarily complex, but hundreds of men and women, who would otherwise have disappeared into prison or ended up on the gallows, were helped to safety by this American Scarlet Pimpernel. Though this appealed very much to the romantic streak in Dulles's makeup, it hardly ranked in importance with the kind of work he was doing during the war, when, at various stages, he was plotting with the German military opposition or with Himmler's aides the assassination of Hitler, or organizing the surrender of the German army in Italy. Dulles saw himself as a mover of mountains and a creator of empires. Intelligence was war by other means, a creative instrument of American policy. The free world had a duty to the satellite countries: to rescue them from the maw of Joseph Stalin. Yet war was unthinkable. There had to be, and there was, another way. So Dulles set out to find it.

Somehow America's secret intelligence services had to be reactivated. They had to be used to infiltrate the satellites and destroy them from within. Dulles knew instinctively that he was best qualified to handle the job. With the aid of prominent Republicans, he set about the task of capturing for himself the Central Intelligence Agency. Since he stood no chance under the Democrats, he pinned his flag to the masthead of Governor Thomas E. Dewey.

By the beginning of 1948 he—and everyone else in the know—believed that he had fulfilled his ambition. Governor Dewey, as everyone knew, was about to sweep Harry S. Truman, that little man from Missouri, out of the White House in the November elections. The new Republican administration, dedicated to combating communism at home and abroad, would cleanse Washington of the New Dealers. John Foster Dulles would get the State Department; his younger brother, Allen Welsh Dulles, the newly founded CIA.

Even President Truman, confident he would win the election despite the polls and opinions, seemed to be infected by the possibility of defeat. Accepting a bipartisan foreign policy, he agreed that Allen Dulles should be properly prepared for the awesome responsibility which Dewey had in hand for him. In asking Dulles to chair a committee*

---

* On the committee with Dulles were two senior members of the American intelligence establishment, William H. Jackson, who had served in wartime military intelligence, and Mathias F. Correa, who had been a special assistant to the secretary of the Navy.

to report on the National Security Act and the various intelligence organizations in the government, Truman was in effect giving him a year-long apprenticeship in the workings and methods of an agency which he would head after Dewey's inauguration. Dulles had no need to conceal his political leanings; even while he was in theory working for President Truman, chairing an important committee, looking into potentially one of the most powerful organs of American foreign policy, he was also one of Governor Dewey's chief advisers and speech writers.

Considering the importance of the Dulles committee, it was a peculiar situation, one which appealed to Dulles's rather wicked sense of humor. But so certain was everyone that Harry Truman was a lame-duck president, that it was approved. Dewey was right to assemble his administration early on; these were dangerous years and there was little time for political niceties.

Dulles took the job handed him by the president very seriously. He saw it as an opportunity, no more and no less, to write his own job description, and he set his sights suitably high. In a few months' time, the agency would be his, and it had to be an agency capable of fulfilling the role he envisaged for it in a troubled world.

The Dulles report remains a classified document and only its general outline is known. It argued that a secret war was being waged around the world by the Soviet Union and that America was in danger of losing it by default. America lacked an efficient organization to collect and analyze even material in the public domain, much less secret information from a potentially hostile power.

The report stated that the traditional role of intelligence, such as the collection of military data and the theft of another country's industrial and scientific secrets, was of minor importance as far as the United States was concerned. It was pointless to mount an expensive and dangerous operation to discover, for example, the thickness of armor on the latest Russian tank when the Americans were developing shells which would penetrate anything within current scientific knowledge.

What America needed was political intelligence. She had to have an operation which could detect the political currents heralding a military threat in time to face up to the challenge. Evaluation of information was all-important, and there had to be a staff and a budget large enough to handle it.

But the Central Intelligence Agency must not be merely a passive recipient of Iron Curtain intelligence; it must go out and challenge the Communist menace on its own home ground. It must be equipped to mount large-scale sophisticated covert political operations designed to destroy Stalin's grip on the satellites and turn back the tide of communism. The satellites, slave states all, must be encouraged to rise up and throw off the yoke of the oppressor. The mission of the CIA must be to create the conditions to make that possible. The director himself, said Dulles, should be answerable only to the president; he should be a high-ranking civilian with the authority of an army chief of staff to wage a secret war against America's enemies.

The Dulles proposals went far beyond what Congress had accepted when it passed the National Security Act in July 1947, bringing the CIA into being. The NSA, whose authors were mindful that a powerful CIA director might have too great an influence upon U.S. policy, established a National Security Council, consisting of the president, the vice-president, the secretary of defense and the director of the Office of Emergency Planning, to whom he was to be directly responsible. The council, not the CIA director, would sit at the apex of American intelligence. The primary function of the new agency was merely "coordinating the intelligence activities of the several government departments and agencies."

A potentially more sinister clause written into the act permitted the agency "to perform such other functions and duties related to intelligence affecting the national security as the NSC may from time to time direct." Once the agency had been established, the NSC gave this specific meaning by stating that the CIA had strictly limited authority "to carry through clandestine operations which the NSC directed" and stipulated that these must be truly clandestine and capable of being disclaimed by the U.S. government. Though these provisions did elevate the agency from a mere collection and coordination center to an operational unit, those who framed the original act and those who drafted the subsequent NSA addendum were careful to place not only the power of veto upon the NSC but to establish the NSC as the fountainhead from which all operational orders would flow. In other words, the director of the CIA was not envisaged as a policy maker, and it was precisely that provision which Dulles was now fighting. No secret agency run on the lines which he believed necessary could possibly work if its director was so circumscribed by law.

But in the field of espionage, only those in possession of highly restricted and secret information can be expected to reach the right conclusions as to what policy line to adopt in the face of a piece of new intelligence. Should the director of the CIA, whose job it is to present to the NSC the information from which it is then expected to draw a conclusion, bend his presentation even a little, the NSC cannot be blamed if it arrives at a policy decision for which the agency has been angling. To take a not entirely apocryphal example: the director wants more funds in order to increase his East German establishment. He persuades the NSC that the Soviets are building up in strength for some unfathomable purpose in East Berlin. It will be the NSC who will then suggest extra men and extra funds, not the director of the CIA.

But Dulles wanted more than the ability to manipulate the NSC. He felt the director should be free from all legal incumbrances as well. But he was never interested in power for power's sake. He was socially agreeable and professionally honest with his associates. He was an ambitious man but not a megalomaniac. He did see communism, however, as a worldwide menace and believed only his methods would defeat and destroy it. And in 1948, thanks to his position on the Dewey campaign staff and his appointment as chairman of the Select Committee on the workings of the CIA, he was in a remarkable position. Allen Dulles represented all power and no accountability.

Work on the report took him into every section of the CIA: he could demand files, see details of operations, interview officers and agents, sit in on staff meetings. Most important of all, because it was believed that he was to be the next director, he could influence policy decisions. Most of the young lions inside the CIA saw eye to eye with Dulles on every point. They too wanted excitement; they shared Dulles's enthusiasm for what he called "dirty tricks" as well as his lack of interest in the more prosaic jobs of evaluation and administration. Many of them had known him during the war, when he had been in Switzerland, and with him resented the treatment meted out to OSS Director Donovan, who had been shunted into retirement after the war and was now stumping the country warning of the "Red menace."

Furthermore, it would not have been possible for Dulles and his two colleagues to prepare a report for the

president on the workings of the CIA if they themselves
were not active, payrolled senior officials of the American
intelligence establishment. The president, perhaps even
the chairman of the Joint Chiefs, the secretary of defense
and the secretary of state, would have security clearance;
but it would go lower to only a small, very select group of
people. The sensitivity of material handled by an intelligence agency is so acute that no outsider, no matter what
his past record, would be permitted access to it. Dulles was
then, and remained until the day he died, an active intelligence operator whose cover in the forties was the firm of
Sullivan & Cromwell and in the fifties the directorship of
the CIA. (I maintain that his directorship was also a very
subtle cover for his primary role as CIA head of special
operations.)

All of this was, of course, known to the professionals in
Britain's SIS. They knew that in dealing with him they
would be able to get American cooperation and at the same
time keep the approach unofficial rather than on the
secret-service or government level. It made for the kind of
arrangement intelligence agencies like. So it was that Allen
Dulles greeted his British visitor in his book-lined Wall
Street office with all the outward signs of cordiality.
Puffing at his pipe, his eyes twinkling from behind his rim-
less spectacles, comfortably, if, in the circumstances, somewhat eccentrically dressed in a vest and carpet slippers, he
looked like a college professor dealing in the unworldly
realism of medieval English, rather than the professional
spy master he actually was.

Though he tried not to show it, Dulles never liked the
British. As a precocious eight-year-old, he had published
his first work (reviewed in *The New York Times*), a vigor-
ous if poorly spelled denunciation of British policy toward
the Boers during the South African war, and, like many

Americans of his generation, he came to regard the British Empire as a constant threat to international stability.*

But Dulles's natural wariness of his ally quickly evaporated when his visitor from SIS handed him the Swiatlo file and suggested that America might be interested in taking the Polish defector over. He could scarcely conceal his excitement. Only a day or so previously he had looked at the personnel files of American double agents operating inside Eastern Europe, one man more useless than the next. The odd border guard, clerks who were in it to eke out a meager salary, but that was all. The cupboard was embarrassingly, even dangerously, bare. Jozef Swiatlo was the answer to a prayer.†

At that time America had no one to draw on. Yet Dulles had grandiose plans as to how American intelligence should operate in the postwar world. He was a general without an army, a strategist playing a game of make-believe in a sandbox. It was deeply frustrating. Already signs of a crack in the Soviet monolith had appeared when, in June 1948, Yugoslavia was expelled from the Cominform because Marshal Tito refused to sacrifice sovereignty to the Soviet

---

* During World War II his free-wheeling ways in Berne frequently irritated the local SIS people, and from time to time he was regarded as being either too sympathetic to the Nazis negotiating with him or, contrarily, with the Communists who had fled to Switzerland seeking sanctuary from all over occupied Europe. Though he was the first to admit that SIS possessed an experience and expertise which he and America's fledgling intelligence apparatus lacked, he felt that top SIS personnel were often too naïve politically to know what to do with information once they got it. He tended to regard SIS people as possible security risks, and would, when angered, brush them aside as "that bunch of pansies"—ironically echoing the charge leveled by FBI Director J. Edgar Hoover against Dulles's own young men.

† Covert intelligence cannot be arranged overnight. Few operations with a long-term objective have succeeded without first acquiring a man inside the opposition camp, within the intelligence apparatus of the other side. It is more than likely that today the FBI and the CIA have among their senior-level employees an active Russian agent feeding material to Moscow. Both American agencies are aware of this. To protect themselves, they impose a very strict "need to know" rule in order to reduce the potential damage he can cause. It's a situation they have learned to live with.

Union. Apply the lever in the right direction, Dulles believed, and Czechoslovakia, Poland, Bulgaria and all the rest could be persuaded to follow. That should be the prime objective of American intelligence. The CIA must create the conditions which would lead to rebellion in the satellites and prize them loose from Stalin's grip. But even to launch such an operation there had to be men working for him inside Communist Europe who were deeply entrenched in the government and the security services.

He had a mission—to exert the pressure to force political changes in Eastern Europe—and he persuaded the National Security Council that this should be the CIA's foremost priority. Now, by basing his plan initially on this one man, Jozef Swiatlo, he had the chance to build up a network that could make it all possible. Around Swiatlo, Dulles could build up his team. Today he had one security man in his pocket, tomorrow he could have ten and the day after he would have enough to cover the length and breadth of Eastern Europe. Swiatlo had to be hooked.

A special courier was sent to Warsaw to open negotiations with the Pole. He was an experienced man and conducted himself with more aplomb than had been shown by any American agent since the end of World War II.

Swiatlo was asked to remain at his post. His safety would be assured; permanent arrangements to lift him out in an emergency would be set up by an organization with no other function than to update itself every twenty-four hours until needed. A separate network would provide him with all the help he required, from money to communications. He would be more than adequately compensated both immediately and when his work was over, at which time he would be provided with "transport" to the West.

Jozef Swiatlo agreed. The most successful Western agent in the history of the Cold War had been activated, but his work had not yet begun.

Chapter 5

The Pawn

Noel Field had been born in London on January 23, 1904, of an English mother and an American father, Dr. Herbert Field, a distinguished biologist, and was brought up in Zurich, Switzerland. His family were Quakers, and his intellect, his education and his father's contacts seemed to assure him a rosy future in American public service. He went to Harvard and hoped eventually to join the State Department. His sympathies lay with the underdog in a dreamy kind of way, and his left-wing leanings were sharpened by the Sacco-Vanzetti case in 1927. Sacco and Vanzetti, two poor Italians, were almost certainly wrongly convicted and sentenced to death on a charge of armed robbery and murder. The case became one of the great left-wing causes of the day because it was thought the court was affected more by the radical beliefs of the accused than by the crime itself. Exploited by the American Communist party, it represented for Noel Field and many of his contemporaries a political experience of such intensity that it set their radical convictions ablaze; Sacco and Vanzetti personified the poor and underprivileged.

On September 1, 1926, Noel Field entered the State Department as a foreign service officer, but, because he was regarded as politically immature, he was not permitted to go abroad for a few years, not until the State Department had succeeded in rubbing away some of his rougher edges. In 1929, while preparing position papers for the London Conference on Naval Disarmament, he met and worked with a member of the delegation, Allen Dulles. They were men from the same class with similar family backgrounds and educations. Though Dulles was a Republican from a well-known Republican family and Field far to the left of any of the main-line American political parties, they found that in discussing international political affairs they tended to agree.

Then, as now, generational attitudes rather than formal political party lines tended to color people's political thinking. Young men like Field and Dulles were disgusted that America was not a member of the League of Nations and regarded this as a total and unforgivable abdication of her international responsibilities. They talked about the need for world government and disarmament; they felt the American government should start exerting its influence in a world constantly upset by the congenitally troublesome and quarrelsome Europeans.

Noel Field went far beyond that, however. He was involving himself more and more with the radical left, but, in the comparatively relaxed political atmosphere of those days, no one seemed to mind that a State Department employee was working for one left-wing cause after

another. He had almost no friends in the department itself
save for Laurence Duggan, who arrived at Foggy Bottom
in 1930, and, because he and Field were so politically in
tune, was soon sharing a house with Field and his wife,
Herta.

Climbing the ladder of promotion rapidly, Noel Field
had by 1930 become senior economic adviser of the Western European Affairs Division, and he threw himself into
his work and his extracurricular activities with zest. When
President Roosevelt won the 1933 election and ushered in
the period of the New Deal, Washington was a marvelous
place to live. Everything and anything seemed possible.

Noel Field had as a new friend a lawyer in the Department of Agriculture, Alger Hiss. In her book *The Man
Who Disappeared*, Flora Lewis has described the friendship:

> The two couples, Hiss and Field, took to each other
> immediately. To Alger, Noel seemed rather British "and
> that appealed to me." Hiss was attracted by the quiet
> grave manner, the obvious culture, of the tall and
> slightly stooping Noel Field. Very quickly, they took up
> a family relationship. Alger Hiss's wife, Priscilla, slipped
> into a comfortable Quaker "thee" and "thou" when she
> spoke to Noel and the four of them gathered together for
> family dinners. When they went to Hiss's house, the
> Fields would fuss over and pamper the children, whom
> they admired immensely. Along with the Duggans, who
> remained the Fields' best friends, they were a close and
> easy group with many common interests. Alger was the
> quick, witty one, who always landed on his feet, always
> seemed to feel at home. Larry Duggan was the lucid, rea-
> soned one, practical and incisive. Noel was the sensitive
> one, learned but unsure of himself. He admired his friends
> with all his heart, as he always admired people with self-
> confidence.

All of them were caught up with the feeling of worlds amaking that pervaded Washington, a thrilling sense of importance of being midwives at the birth of a new and better society.*

It was, of course, the Left who reacted in this way, who misunderstood Roosevelt and who adopted increasingly extreme attitudes. For Noel Field, who at this stage had not even considered becoming a member of the Communist party, it might all have ended there, as it did for thousands of others—an innocent flirtation with Communist ideals occasioned by a world where the choice appeared to be between an uncaring capitalism with its ugly offspring, fascism, and the militant socialism which only Soviet Russia could offer to combat it.

Many young people from privileged homes, especially those as sensitive as Noel Field, could not help but compare their own well-being with the evils of poverty and economic exploitation which they saw all around them. The difference between them and a man like Field was one of degree. Perhaps all that Field lacked was a thin coating of healthy cynicism. He was a political baby in a world of adults.

This childlike quality in Field, occasionally so appealing, began to take on a more sinister aspect in the mid-thirties. He and his wife, along with many others, were deeply moved by Paul Massing's article in the American left-wing periodical *New Masses* on his imprisonment and torture by the Nazis in Germany. The German Communist's story was one of the first complete eyewitness accounts of what the Gestapo was up to in its "work camps," and it provided confirmation of what the Left had been claiming all along in its propaganda about the Nazis.

* Flora Lewis, *The Man Who Disappeared* (London: Arthur Barker Ltd., 1965), pp. 58–59.

When Noel heard that the author's wife was in New York, he asked her to dinner. He was not to know that Hede Massing was a Soviet agent whose brief was to recruit as agents members of the American intelligentsia, especially those in the government. It was decided, after her fortuitous initial contact with Field, that he would be her primary target.

By 1935 Field's left-wing convictions had, in fact, boiled over, and he decided openly to join the American Communist party. Hede Massing's first job was to try to persuade him not to do so. As a senior State Department employee, he was of enormous potential use to the Russians. But if he joined the party, he would have to resign his post and, as far as the Russians were concerned, he would lose all value as an informant. There is evidence that Noel Field did apply for party membership, but this was rejected by the leader of the American Communist party, Earl Browder, on, it is believed, instructions from Moscow. The rejection hurt Field deeply and he never forgave Browder for what he regarded as a slur on his character.

Meanwhile, Hede Massing and her husband, Paul, who had managed to get to America from Germany, worked on Field almost day and night to persuade him that he should remain in a position to assist the cause for "international peace" by passing classified information out of the State Department for onward transmission to Moscow. Field balked. He talked about loyalty to his country and the trust placed in him by his superiors, but he was an easy target for such an experienced and highly trained agent as Hede Massing.

In the thirties a good many men like Field took the view that fascism was so evil that anything was justified to defeat it. It was holy writ among all "progressives" that one day Hitler would attack Russia and that the resulting war would be nothing less than a battle for civilization itself. In light of this, Noel Field came to believe that he had a higher duty than that of loyalty to the State Department: he had a duty to humanity.

There were many contradictions in the character of this complex man. Though he spoke foreign languages fluently and longed to be posted abroad, he felt he belonged in America and was a part of all things American. He solved this dilemma between, as he saw it, his two duties in a typically naïve manner. He did give Hede Massing documents, but he made sure that they were not of any real importance and could not damage his country. It was a situation which could not last for long. If he had started off by merely handing over the canteen menu, he would have become a cat's-paw in the thrall of a vicious, unbelieving espionage apparatus.

But Noel Field occasionally showed a steely backbone. He realized quickly that he had taken the first step to treason, and, in order to avoid harming his country further, made a courageous move that was damaging both to his professional life as a State Department official and to his relations with his new Russian masters. The latter never forgave him.

In 1936 two job opportunities presented themselves to him. The first was as a member of the League of Nations secretariat in Geneva, and the second as officer in charge of the German desk at the State Department. Even though he believed passionately in the work of the League, he could see that it would soon evaporate altogether. The German desk was, however, not only a major promotion but an opportunity for him to deal with the one country in the world which he regarded as a threat to civilization. From there, he could exert an influence upon American policy. It has been suggested that he turned down the job because at the time it would have involved helping set up a new American-German trade agreement and dealing with German diplomats in Washington "diplomatically"—functions he would have been constitutionally incapable of performing. It is hard to believe that his State Department training had not left upon him its mark: the ability to perform a public function while all the time arguing against it effectively in private.

As far as the Russians and Hede Massing's instructions were concerned, there was no question which job he should take. A Russian agent running the German desk at the State Department would have been a coup of quite exceptional significance, producing almost unbelievable dividends. Field would have become one of the most important Russian agents in the Western world. The pressure upon him to accept the assignment reached remarkable intensity. Yet, in April 1936, Noel Field suddenly announced that he felt he had a moral obligation to work for the League, packed his bags and sailed for Geneva.

There is no record of what actually motivated him to turn down the German desk. It may have been an excessive sense of idealism, but the facts suggest the contrary. Noel Field was deliberately deciding against becoming a full-fledged Russian agent, knowing by that time that if he remained in Washington, he was hooked. Just as it was impossible for him to be a loyal and conscientious member of the State Department staff, so it was impossible for him to run the German desk without handing over to the Russians every confidential and secret telegram which passed through his hands. He was neither emotionally equipped to handle such conflicts of loyalty nor tough enough to be what he would have to become: a Soviet spy.

In rejecting Russian demands to take the job, Field—who, by that time, must have known something about the reality of Soviet power—knew that he was disobeying orders from a master who did not take such lapses lightly. In Switzerland, and at the League, already overrun by Russian agents, he would be all but useless. The call had come and he had rejected it. He was never forgiven for it by the Russians and, at the same time, he was never excused by the Americans for his previous activities. Throughout his life, he carried upon his shoulders the burden of a twin guilt—that he had betrayed both his country and his cause. For a man like Field, that was not as easy belief to live with.

But perhaps after all these years an expression of grudging respect is due him. Few men, trapped by the Russian secret service through stupidity, naïveté or greed, have managed to extricate themselves sufficiently to avoid the major betrayal. Field did so; it was an act of courage and loyalty to the American flag.

Probably only a man like Noel Field could find the work of the moribund League of Nations exciting, but that he did. Indeed, it did become genuinely so when in 1938 he was appointed secretary of the League Commission set up to supervise the repatriation of foreigners who had come from all over the world to fight on the side of the Loyalists and who were about to be overrun by the already victorious General Francisco Franco during the Spanish civil war. It was the real thing—fascism against the forces of democracy—and Noel Field, who performed valiantly in channeling relief to the pathetic detritus of the international Left who had flocked so nobly and yet so futilely to Spain, was deeply moved by what he saw. For once Field felt truly useful. It was work he could do and do well. The war clouds were gathering, and there would be more refugees to help. Noel Field had come to Europe and found his mission.

Once war broke out, Allen Dulles, the man he had briefly met some years earlier, had found his mission too. Dulles arrived in Berne in 1942 ostensibly as a member of the American legation, but in actuality he was in charge of the Swiss sector of the OSS—a vital intelligence head-quarters in a neutral country in the middle of war-torn Europe.* Simultaneously, from 1942 on, he was negotiating at a higher level with the Germans with certainly more success than any other individual on the Allied side. Noel Field was an important man too. In 1941 he had been appointed resident American director of the Unitarian Services Committee office in Marseilles in Vichy France, where, with selfless energy, he looked after the countless refugees who were packing the city. But in November 1942, as the Nazis decided to occupy all of France, Noel and Herta Field dramatically fled to Switzerland in the last train to leave the country. In Geneva Noel was ap-pointed European director of the Unitarian Services mis-sion, and soon the Unitarians became the most important single relief agency in Europe, and Noel himself one of the most influential Americans in Switzerland.

The paths of the two men would almost certainly have crossed in any case, but the first meeting since the days they worked together in the State Department in the thir-ties was precipitated by Dr. Robert Dexter. In 1940 the

* He did not bother to acknowledge his cover role as a staff diplo-mat. Rather, he gloried in his role as an American spy master and wanted everyone to know about it. In Switzerland there was an intelli-gence case for him to be out in the open. The country was swarming with agents (there were representatives of all the different German cliques in residence: straight Nazis, anti-Nazi Germans, pro-Nazi, anti-Hitler Germans, German Communists, Germans who wanted to negotiate a reasonable settlement to the war and others with their own ideas), and Dulles quite correctly took the view that he should become the magnet which would draw these conflicting interests toward him, clearly an impossibility if he remained under cover. In a sense, it was a curious role—that of a clandestine agent whose identity and job were known to one and all.

Unitarians had sent for Dr. Dexter to examine the refugee situation in Europe and report on the opportunities for humanitarian services. It was his report describing the terrible ravages of the war which persuaded the Unitarians to set up their relief mission. Dexter was appointed Lisbon director of the mission, of which Noel Field's post, Marseilles, was, at least initially, an outstation. While doing this job, Dexter was also an undercover member of the OSS, answerable to Allen Dulles in Berne. As so frequently in Noel Field's life, a chance set of circumstances seemed to dominate everything that happened to him.

Dexter reintroduced Field to Dulles in Berne with the clear intention of recruiting him into the OSS; Field could, as Dexter himself was doing, use the Unitarian Services mission as a cover. Dexter suggested that the many refugees flowing through Field's camps from all over occupied Europe, East as well as West, could provide an inexhaustible fund of intelligence for the OSS.

At this stage in his life, Field was desperately seeking to mend fences with the Communists and, under a cover name, had become a candidate for membership in the Swiss Communist party. He knew, however, that his suitability would be determined by Moscow and that it was Moscow he would have to impress if he was ever to get back into good favor. The problem was that because of wartime conditions the Swiss party was operating on purely local military intelligence and was thus virtually out of contact with "political Moscow," which was where Field needed assistance. He had no way of knowing that any decision made in his favor would be a local one only, unlikely to help him when Moscow got back into the picture, and indeed it could be open to the most horrendous misunderstandings.

This need to impress the Communists had produced at

least one result which was to his grave discredit. Refugees were accepted by the Unitarians not strictly on the basis of need but on whether or not they had been recommended by the party. This is not to say that the Communists of Europe did not need as much assistance as anyone else— they were, after all, appallingly persecuted by the Nazis and, if caught, were bound for the living death of a concentration camp. Equally, the Spanish civil war had produced in southern Europe a great many refugee camps of Communists or fellow travelers who had fought on the Republican side, lost and now had nowhere to go. Nevertheless, the Unitarians in Boston had no idea that the aid they provided with the help of public subscription and fund raising in America was being used to assist, by and large, only members of the Communist party and that non-Communists, especially vocal anti-Communists, were rigidly excluded from the Unitarian camps.

But Dexter, and through him Allen Dulles, recognized that Field's refugees tended to be "politicals." They did not regard this as particularly sinister or even unusual. If by chance the first people he helped happened to be veterans from the Spanish civil war, it would be fairly natural for their friends to gravitate toward him. But this situation did make Field's refugees potentially useful: politically aware, they were perhaps better informed and sharper observers than most others.

Determined not to get himself into more trouble with the Communists, Field put the Dexter-Dulles request to assist the OSS to Leo Bauer, head of the German Communists in Switzerland, as Germany was clearly the area in which Dulles was principally interested. The Germans agreed to help in return for American money to finance their own "anti-Fascist crusade." Field brought Leo Bauer to Dulles to discuss the issue, and the two men quickly came to an understanding. In the meantime, other Communist groups which Field approached agreed to help too, but again against a cash consideration, which Dulles, with great largesse, distributed through Field.*

Meanwhile, Field was going from strength to strength. Aside from its function as a passive collection center for refugees from all over Europe, his Unitarian relief mission, from its Geneva base, also was involved in actively lifting important people out of occupied Europe to safety. Regular couriers, including occasionally his wife, Herta, went into occupied Europe, passing and receiving messages, principally from Communists. Field himself reveled in the work, combining as it did his romantic need to be where the action was, his humanitarian beliefs and his fairly highly developed taste for intrigue.

By 1943 his problems, as far as the Russians were concerned, seemed to be over. He must have thought he was getting indirect encouragement from Moscow when a message from Wilhelm Pieck, a German Communist who was subsequently to become the first president of East Germany, sent to Jules Humbert Droz, the veteran leader of the Swiss Communist party and an international figure, a

---

* It was a cosy relationship that was nearly upset when Dexter approached Leo Bauer one day with a man known only as Fred. Dexter asked Bauer to take away a questionnaire regarding detailed military information the OSS required on Germany. Bauer took the form—which clearly emanated from an espionage outfit—away with him but was promptly arrested by the Swiss police for having incorrect identification papers. Unluckily, the questionnaire was in his briefcase. If the Swiss, who because of their neutral status were careful not to permit any military espionage operations to be conducted behind their borders, had even suspected that this form found on a German Communist had initially come from Dulles, he would almost certainly have been declared *persona non grata* and thrown out of the country. But Bauer refused to reveal the identity of the man who had given it to him and obeyed Dulles's terse instruction, relayed to him in prison through a third person, to "keep your mouth shut." He was subsequently acquitted of being a spy but nevertheless was sent to an internment camp for various other offenses against Swiss federal law.

list of German Communists whom Field should try to
rescue from France. It was a remarkable acknowledgment
of what Field had achieved and was thought capable of
achieving in the future.

Simultaneously he was providing invaluable information for Allen Dulles, not only about conditions inside the
occupied territories but in Germany as well. Throughout
the war the Communists were probably the only disciplined opposition party to the Nazis, ready, like their oppo-
nents, to take and receive orders and act as a coherent
political resistance force instead of spending the time arguing incessantly among themselves. This meant that anyone
with a direct line to the Communists knew he was dealing
with a group of dedicated professionals who had both the
means and the will to come up with what was required.
Until Allen Dulles plugged himself into Noel Field, this
tremendous potential source of information had been
almost completely disregarded—a situation which was as
wasteful for the Communists as it was for Western war
planners. There can be little doubt that Field and Dulles
between them produced a steady stream of accurate information for the Allies, and that, as a result, Berne became
one of the most important Allied intelligence collection
centers during the war.*

However, the Field–Dulles relationship changed
drastically toward the end of the war, when Field made
Dulles an unwitting dupe of the Communists. After the

---

* One of Field's finds almost certainly altered American policy
toward national resistance movements. At the time, America was helping the Draza Mihailovic resistance to the Germans in Yugoslavia at
the expense of the Tito forces. All this changed when Field introduced
to Dulles two important Yugoslavian Communists who managed to
persuade Dulles that only they were strong and self-disciplined enough
to take the Nazis on and finally defeat them. Dulles was sold on the
idea and persuaded the military to switch its support to Tito. It was
an important turning point for Tito and for the entire anti-Nazi coalition in Eastern Europe.

fall of Stalingrad the Russians formed, with the help of captured German generals, a "Free Germany Committee," which was designed to be the nucleus of a Communist government in Germany after the war under Walter Ulbricht, who was biding out his time in Moscow. Later, after the liberation of Paris, a Western branch was established in France and Switzerland under the name of CALPO (Comité de l'Allemagne Libre Pour l'Ouest). It was clearly a Communist-front organization.

In December Field came to Dulles with an idea which Dulles grasped at instantly. As the American and British armies advanced through Germany, it became essential not only to establish orderly administration in their wake, but also to have agents in position waiting for the advancing Allied troops and preparing the way for them. Equally, it was realized that many *Wehrmacht* commanders, knowing that the war was lost in any case, could be persuaded to surrender locally in advance of the fall of Berlin, thus saving lives and time. Field suggested that CALPO and its contacts be used for this task and that CALPO provide a steady stream of agents who could be parachuted or taken into Germany by some other means. Dulles was enthusiastic and told Field to talk to the OSS office in Paris, where CALPO had its headquarters. The man Field met was Arthur Schlesinger, Jr., then only twenty-seven years old, and who, with the supreme self-confidence of youth, was able to do what Allen Dulles had failed to do all those years: he saw through Noel Field at a glance. "What struck me most was his self-righteous stupidity. He was a Quaker Communist, filled with smugness and self-sacrifice and not a very intelligent man," Schlesinger declared.* Paris rejected the plan but, despite this, Allen Dulles did

---

* R. Harris Smith, *O.S.S.: The Secret History of America's First Central Intelligence Agency* (Berkeley, Calif.: University of California Press, 1972), p. 228.

go through with it, using people whom Field suggested rather than direct CALPO nominees. It was, of course, one and the same thing.

So in Germany, Hungary, Yugoslavia and Czechoslovakia, Communists—backed by the OSS, sometimes provided with American army uniforms, supported with American money, for several months given all of the benefits of wearing the colors of the victor—were able to get their hands on the reins of power long before the non-Communist democratic forces were able to regroup and organize themselves.

Shortly after the end of the war, this was one joke which intelligence services, both in the East and the West, could appreciate and did. It was rubbed in by the fact that the OSS under Dulles's direction, again with Field's help, had published and distributed inside Germany a clandestine newspaper, anti-Fascist and left-wing, and supposedly produced by a left-wing underground in Germany. The newspaper was given the title *Neues Deutschland,* which immediately upon liberation became the official newspaper of the East German Communist party.

The joke was very much on Dulles. The intelligence world is a small one, and it doesn't take long for a story of this kind to get around and for capital to be made out of it. Dulles had been duped by a man who, as everyone was now telling him, was a known Communist. He felt that Field had betrayed the trust he had shown in him. The fact that Field had procured first-class raw intelligence for the Allied cause was forgotten in the light of the evidence that, in the closing minutes of the war, he had managed to twist the tail of the OSS and embarrass severely its most dashing executive, Allen Welsh Dulles. He had shown that the Communists were his real masters and that for them he was prepared to betray his own country.

Dulles did not forgive and did not forget.

In January of 1949 Noel Field stepped off a plane at Warsaw's Okecie Airport and into the arms of waiting friends who greeted him with that deep affection which people reserve for each other after they have been through common experiences of danger and suffering.

He stooped slightly, and the hair brushed back off his high forehead set off his large pale eyes and his generous, if slightly weak, mouth. He seemed both excited and nervous, for he believed this trip would be the making or breaking of him.

January is no time to visit Warsaw—especially that January. Both the political temperature and the weather were well below freezing point. The Berlin blockade was at its height, and everywhere, in both the East and West, people talked nervously of war. In Warsaw posters exhorted the people to prepare for the worst. German militarists were rampant and the wolves of international capitalism on the rampage. Comrades to arms!

If Noel Field thought these exhortations even mildly hysterical, he gave no sign of it. There were many people like him in the thirties and forties, men and women with inquiring minds and highly developed critical faculties whose one blind spot was their failure to see how Marxist communism had been brutally and cynically warped by Joseph Stalin and those who supported him. Heirs of a great Western liberal tradition, they shut their eyes to the Communists' absolute rejection of every liberal standard, such as freedom of speech, the importance of the individual, fair trials, an independent judiciary, habeas corpus. Everyone in the world knew Stalinism meant the dawn arrest, the torture of political prisoners, labor camps, where thousands died—everyone save for people like Noel Field.

For a forty-five-year-old man who once had had a most distinguished career stretching out before him, 1949

seemed like the end of the road. Noel Field had just lost his
job as head of the Unitarian relief mission in Europe
because he had turned this fine charitable foundation with
its headquarters in Boston into little more than a Communist-front organization. His friend, Larry Duggan, suspected of being a Communist, had died after falling from
the sixteenth floor of his office onto New York's Fifth
Avenue. As in the case of Masaryk, no one knew whether
he had jumped or was pushed—and if pushed, by whom.
Alger Hiss was being investigated by Congress, and not
only had Noel Field been mentioned during the testimony,
but he would almost certainly be subpoenaed as a witness
if he ever returned to the United States. Noel Field was in
Warsaw, in effect, to arrange his political asylum—to change
sides and allegiances.

Much had happened to Noel Field from the time he
left the State Department in 1946 to go to Geneva until his
arrival in Poland on that cold January of 1949. He was
considered a Communist spy by the Americans and was
regarded with immense suspicion by the Communists; he
knew he had to burn his bridges completely with the
former in order to reestablish the confidence of the latter.

Nevertheless, his arrival in Warsaw in 1949 excited the
attention of the Bezpieka, the Polish secret police. A few
months earlier he had been on a similar mission to Prague
—looking for a job—and Czech security placed his name
on the "gray file," which contained details of people who
bore watching but against whom nothing had been established. It was decided that he would not be permitted to
work or live in Prague, and his file was forwarded to other
countries inside Eastern Europe as a routine precaution.
That Field's name was on the "gray file" was not particularly unusual or likely to cause him any problems or
embarrassment in the future. (Most journalists, business-

men and diplomats who visit Eastern Europe are similarly
tagged and never have cause to know it.)

The Polish police were, however, particularly interested because they had a similar file on Noel Field's
brother, Hermann, who had visited Warsaw in 1948 as the
head of a delegation of American architects. Before the war
he had worked in Katowice for the British Trust, an organization set up by the British Liberal peer Lord Layton
to help hundreds of Czechs, mainly Communists, leave their
country after the German invasion. By 1948 the British
Trust had been established within the imagination of the
Polish secret police as a front for British intelligence, and
Hermann Field, who had many friends in Warsaw, indeed
throughout Poland and Czechoslovakia, was regarded with
the gravest suspicion.

That Noel Field had spent the war working for a similar organization in Europe, the American Unitarians—also
a likely front for Western espionage, and which also
brought him into daily contact with senior Communist
party officials—struck the Bezpieka as an improbable coincidence. Before his visa was granted, the Bezpieka had
asked every other country in the Communist bloc for more
information about this curious man. The results of their
inquiries were quite staggering.

Noel Field seemed to know almost everyone worth
knowing in the whole of Eastern Europe. He was on first-
name terms with members of the Politburo of Poland,
Hungary, Czechoslovakia, East Germany, Bulgaria and
Yugoslavia; he knew ministers and sent them cards of congratulations upon their appointments. He had established
leading Communists in Poland, Czechoslovakia and Hungary as local representatives for the Unitarians. One condition for this aid was that the local representatives from
time to time send reports concerning the economic condi-

tions of the regions for which the aid was destined—a condition which could, in the political circumstances of those
days, have most damning connotations.

Even more disturbing, an attractive young girl, Erica
Glaser Wallach, down on the records as Noel Field's
adopted daughter (though, in fact, she was not), had once
been a member of the German Communist party; she had
since left the party, but still had friends inside the East
German Politburo.

In a period of history when contacts between East
Europeans and Westerners were severely discouraged, here
was a man who knew, or had family who knew, literally
hundreds of leading Communists throughout the bloc. And
now his attempts to find a job in Eastern Europe made
him an object of the profoundest suspicion.

It would have been impossible, however, not to grant
him a visa, considering the great need then to rally Western Communists and "progressives" to the cause. To have
refused a man like Noel Field a visit to one of the people's
democracies with no good reason would have caused a serious upset among Western liberals. So, not without misgiv-
ings, he was permitted to come to Poland.

The surveillance on him during his visit was aggressive
and uncompromising, and reports on him were circulated
to all departments of the Bezpieka. In this way Colonel
Jozef Swiatlo heard about him for the first time. Department 10, of course, was more than interested in the case. If
Field was an American spy, then Communists who had
been or were in contact with him would be of the greatest
interest to the department. If, as the Russians seemed to
claim, he was a Trotskyist, then his Polish contacts would
merit equal observation. The Polish Communists who
knew Field were quick to appreciate Bezpieka interest, and
all, save one, presented the UB with details of their rela-

tions with Field in the past in order to clear themselves in
advance against any future investigation.

The one person who didn't do so, probably because she
felt that her position provided its own protection, was an
attractive woman in her early forties who had a distinguished record as a Communist activist before the war and
had worked with Field in Switzerland during the war. Her
name was Anna Duracz, secretary to the all-powerful
Jakub Berman, head of security.

Field saw Anna several times during his Polish trip.
Having complete confidence in him, she told him that he
would have to obtain Russian approval before he could get
a job in Poland—or anywhere else in Eastern Europe—and
offered to help him make contact. Acting on her advice,
Noel Field wrote Jakub Berman, asking him to use his
good offices in establishing for Field some contact with the
Russians. Anna Duracz delivered the letter to Berman,
assuring him she would vouch for the American.

One telephone call to the Bezpieka was sufficient to
persuade Berman that Noel Field was a man to be kept at
arm's length. Nevertheless, out of a sense of courtesy to
Anna Duracz, Berman did reply, telling Field as noncom-
mittally as possible that he would pursue the matter—
without, of course, having any intention of so doing, and
probably hoping that Field would be sensible enough to
read between the lines and let the matter rest. Field had
many talents, but reading between the lines was not one of
them. Nevertheless, he accepted the advice proffered him
by Anna Duracz (who by now was also aware of secret-police interest) that he might as well go on to Prague, the
next stop on his itinerary, and then home to Geneva,
because the whole operation would take time. If there was
any news, she would let him know.

So Noel Field left Warsaw, his hopes high. So sure was

he that he'd be back that he left behind a suitcase full of possessions, mostly books, for his return. But he'd left behind something else, something which was destined to destroy not only himself and his family but the very best of East European communism. Insignificant events have shaped the course of history before, but there can be few occasions where anything so trivial as a begging letter from anyone quite so unimportant as Noel Field can ever have affected the course of nations to such an extent or sparked off a bloodbath of such enormity.

Jozef Swiatlo had started work. Ever since his abortive attempt a year earlier to depose Berman, he had not forgotten his enmity toward this powerful man or his desire to see him destroyed. He continued building up a dossier against Berman—including the fact that the minister's brother-in-law, a doctor, was selling scarce drugs on the black market, and, it was alleged, passing some of the proceeds to Berman—but he still did not have the evidence with which to hang him.

Through a Department 10 operative working in Berman's office Swiatlo heard of the letter concerning Noel Field which Berman had received from his trusted confidante, Anna Duracz. Spy neurosis was at its height; the supercharged imagination of the East European secret police had acted upon less evidence in the past to establish an espionage link between a trusted Communist and the Americans. The letter could be presented as a simple code: references to an introduction to "Soviet colleagues" could be interpreted as a direct invitation to Berman to recruit Russians into the Field network.

One thing had to be established first: Noel Field had to be an American spy. But that would not be difficult for a man in the position which Swiatlo enjoyed—with the enormous panoply of secret-police resources at his command, with a string of informers in prison and out who could be induced one way or the other to provide "confessions" regarding a conspiracy involving Noel Field, and, above all, with a deep knowledge and understanding of the kind of details which would make a charge of this kind stick with the Russians. Swiatlo was at last in the position he had been seeking for so long: the chance to destroy Berman. The letter could be turned into a formidable weapon.

Only one thought stopped him from acting immediately. Swiatlo was by then an American agent. He could not denounce Noel Field as a U.S. spy without first checking with Washington. For chances were that Noel Field *was* working for the Central Intelligence Agency. In that case, Swiatlo's new masters would not thank him for blowing Field's cover completely.

Jozef Swiatlo sent his first message to his controllers in Washington: great damage could be done to the party and party credibility within the country as a whole if Berman could be exposed as actively collaborating with Noel Field, an American agent. Others, too, could be implicated. The message ended "Any objections?"—and Swiatlo sat back and waited.

Chapter 6

Code Name: Splinter Factor

It was a different Washington, and for Allen Dulles the sky had fallen in. Harry S. Truman had been reelected for another term as president of the United States, wrecking in the process the reputation of every opinion poll and pundit in the country, as well as Dulles's prospects.

The Dulles report on the workings of the CIA submitted to President Truman, but designed for President Dewey, was neatly pigeonholed. Instead of being appointed, as all of Washington believed he would be, the new director of the CIA, Dulles got nothing at all. America now had a strong president who had a personal antipathy to the CIA in particular and to espionage in general. It made the work of the professionals difficult, if not impossible.

What stopped a complete rout of Dulles from any

future involvement in the affairs of the agency was that, during his year's service as director-elect, he had managed to insinuate into key positions men who were subsequently to be known as "the Dulles people." This assured him a continuing influence which would eventually lift him, four years later, into the director's chair.

Meanwhile, he retained his cover as a Wall Street lawyer. Remaining a consultant to the CIA on covert operation, Dulles ranked at about the level of CIA's head of operations—which put him at the pinnacle of the American intelligence establishment, but without a power base from which to operate. It was an unsatisfactory situation which only the presence of "his people" ameliorated.

Jozef Swiatlo remained, of course, Allen Dulles's own baby. The Pole was too valuable to risk on day-to-day operations, and Dulles insisted now that he be kept in cold storage, for twenty years if necessary, until the right operation, big enough to justify all, could be devised. But not everyone in the CIA agreed, and Dulles no longer had the political weight to override these objections.

The truth was that the CIA was in trouble, chiefly because of the almost endemic lack of trust which existed then, and exists today, between the CIA and Britain's SIS. Of the many factors which eventually were to lead to Swiatlo's becoming one of the most important intelligence operatives in modern history, this deep suspicion between the intelligence services of these two allies is unquestionably one.*

* It had been Admiral Hillenkoeter who had insisted that if America was to have—as Allen Dulles had suggested, and through whose influence the National Security Council concurred—a clandestine intelligence arm, then it would be just as well to set this up as quickly as possible. The trouble was, of course, that neither naval thoroughness nor American efficiency could produce quickly an operational unit which normally takes years to build up. Faced with this, Admiral Hillenkoeter proposed that it was expensive, inefficient, sometimes dangerous and usually nonsensical for Britain and America to compete in

It didn't take the real professionals inside the CIA long to conclude that the agents handed over by the British were, at best, so shop-worn and, at worst, blown so wide open that they endangered the lives of any American coming even close. So the CIA found itself in an uncomfortable position: it had a political agreement to engage in subversive operations behind the Iron Curtain but lacked the wherewithal to carry this through without risking disaster and major embarrassment to the United States government.

---

the intelligence field and that they should combine their resources. Hillenkoeter flew to London for talks with Sir Stuart Menzies to put forth a proposition. America should take over from SIS Eastern Europe, in which Britain, through Foreign Secretary Ernest Bevin, had already expressed a diminishing interest, in return for a free hand for the British in the Middle East and a sensible, sharing relationship in the Far East.

The advantages to the Americans were obvious: they could buy themselves into a ready-made British operation and, at the same time, gain exclusive control over an area which looked as if it would become the battleground for a new war in which the U.S. would be involved. The British didn't need much persuasion. They regarded the Middle East as their own playground and were becoming increasingly disturbed at evidence that the Americans were beginning to make their own sandcastles on Mediterranean beaches. So a bargain was struck between the heads of the two services, but it never worked out in practice.

Though Menzies agreed to hand over to Hillenkoeter British networks inside Eastern Europe intact, this happened only in a limited way. Equally, though Hillenkoeter consented to give Britain the Mediterranean, the State Department, whether or not it knew of the agreement, would not have honored it. Coincidentally with the London negotiations, talks were going on among the State Department, the Middle East desk at the CIA and the administration to get increased appropriations to keep the whole area under surveillance, and that meant particularly watching the British.

To this day some American CIA men are bitter about the failure of SIS to deliver the goods inside Eastern Europe, and claim that a lot of lives were needlessly thrown away by Britain's jealously maintaining its structure at the expense of the then impoverished Americans. But it would have been impossible, in fact, for British controllers to hand over to the Americans—for whom they had, with some justification then, little regard as professionals—a host of agents who had entrusted their lives to British controllers and who had the right to expect that their identities would be kept a closely guarded secret of His Majesty's Secret Service.

To the CIA top brass, Jozef Swiatlo and the network built up around him presented the only solid base upon which anything of significance could immediately be built. It was true that since 1945 American intelligence had not been idle, and that some solid foundations had been laid for the future, but in very few areas was there anything approximating the sophistication of what had been established in Poland. Within twelve months, by the beginning of 1950, the picture was to have changed completely, but in 1948, the cupboard was bare.

So pressure mounted within the CIA to release Swiatlo immediately for operations, despite Dulles's insistence that these were not worthy of such a valuable agent. These desperate attempts to find an operation suitable for him represented another link in this complex chain which gave Swiatlo the importance he subsequently possessed.

Then the Swiatlo message arrived asking whether Noel Field was an American agent. Dulles's reaction—one of pleasure and amusement—was colored by his dealings with Field in wartime Europe. The CALPO episode had offended both Dulles's pride and his prestige.

The time had come to settle accounts. Allen Dulles, for some time, had been arguing that the only sensible function of American intelligence inside Eastern Europe was to seek to drive a wedge between the satellites and Moscow. Yugoslavia had proved that, given the right economic and political conditions and a leader strong enough or frightened enough to draw the right conclusions, the monolith could be broken open. The Swiatlo–Field link could be so twisted, Dulles realized, that through it the Soviet empire could be torn apart.

Needing, in any case, to activate Swiatlo, Allen Dulles conceived a plan of operation which would become, as he later told a friend, his biggest success ever. For he saw that the Communist parties of each state inside Eastern Europe were hopelessly split and that the increasing demands of a jealous Stalin, for all their outward expressions of fidelity, had imposed an unbearable strain upon the system. Given the right kind of nudge at the right time, the people of Eastern Europe would rise up and cast off the iron bonds with which Stalin kept them enslaved. The West could not free them; they would have to do it themselves.

Dulles brutally brushed aside the notion of some Western diplomatists that nationalist Communists should be given every support, diplomatic and otherwise, representing, as they did, the best hope for restoring some measure of Western influence behind the Iron Curtain. Instead, he believed that communism could be shown for what it was only through the unrestrained practice of Stalinism. He went even further. The nationalist Communists in the long run were potentially more dangerous to the cause of Western democracy than were the hard-line Stalinists. If the form of communism the "liberals" preached was permitted to gain a foothold within the bloc, then communism would become tolerable.

A successful revolution could occur only if the daily existence of the masses were made so insufferable that their misery, both spiritual and economical, surpassed their fear of the consequences of their actions. The thesis could be expanded: permit a nationalist like Gomulka to come to power in Poland and drastically reduce Russian influence on the country, and communism would suddenly become a respectable force which could sweep all before it in Europe. Surely all that was holding the French and Italian workers back from voting the Communists into power in their countries was the realization among a majority that a vote for communism was a vote for the Russians; by and large, they felt safer under the benign patronage of the United States than the vicious colonialism of the Soviet Union.

The point, to Dulles, was not that Moscow communism was a threat to world peace, but that communism of all kinds was intrinsically bad and had to be destroyed. With blinding clarity he saw how it was to be done, and he ordered a message sent to his man in Warsaw.

Jozef Swiatlo was quite surprised when the reply he had been waiting for was personally delivered by his senior American controller. The task he was given was even more astonishing. He was told that he would not work for the Americans, not provide them with intelligence appreciations, not warn them of political or military developments inside Eastern Europe. Instead, he would do the work which his Polish and his Russian masters were paying him to do.

He would find spies everywhere. He would denounce top party leaders as American agents, and the evidence for such a denunciation would be provided by the Americans themselves. He would uncover a major Trotskyist conspiracy, financed by the United States, which was enveloping every country in Russia's satellite empire. He would prove that Titoism was rampant not only in Poland but in Hungary, Bulgaria, Czechoslovakia, Rumania and East Germany. He would report to Beria himself that the center of that conspiracy, the link man between these traitors and Washington, was a man named Noel Haviland Field, who, Beria was to be told, was the most important American intelligence man in Eastern and Western Europe. He would show how Field had run the most successful American espionage operation during World War II, using the Unitarians as his cover. He would show how Field had used his position to attract members of the Communist party to him and then recruit them as agents. He would show how ever since he had left Harvard, Field had worked for American intelligence, posing as a fellow traveler or a member of the Communist party. He would show how, after the war,

Field had infiltrated his agents into Eastern Europe into top positions in party and government so quickly that the big jobs were seized before the Moscow loyalists had a chance of exerting their strength. He would show how, even now that Field's cover was deepening, the Senate investigation was a sham designed to help Field establish himself inside Eastern Europe. He would show, in short, that Noel Field was bent upon the destruction of the entire Soviet bloc and that, moreover, he was perilously close to achieving his aim.

Swiatlo would become the hammer, Noel Field the nail. Swiatlo did as he was bid, and a report went forward to the Russians, both locally and in Moscow.

The CIA knew full well that the standing order inside the MGB was to check out every report of American intelligence operations with obsessive thoroughness—rather unnecessary in light of the fact that there were so few full-fledged American agents. Indeed, the MGB was troubled by its failure to find many agents of note, for neither Stalin nor Beria were prepared to believe that the reason why few American agents were picked up was because there were very few to pick up. The MGB, affected by Stalin's paranoia and the constant barrage of propaganda from its own press about the danger of American spies, didn't believe this reasoning either; rather, it began to believe that it was dealing with an intelligence apparatus of almost superhuman skill and cunning.

The few agents on the ground assisted this psychosis by sprinkling their areas with nonsensical coded messages, giving the impression of an enormous organization with tentacles reaching into every corner of Eastern European life. Men like "Colonel Bell" (actually the American author Ladislas Farago) went on Radio Free Europe night after night, relaying instructions to an enormous army of agents who simply didn't exist outside his own imagination. Every time a train crashed or a fire was reported in the press, Colonel Bell went on the air to congratulate his men on the success of their latest sabotage mission. Ironic as it may seem, the CIA has never again enjoyed such a high reputation from its opposition since those days in the mid-forties, when it hardly existed at all!

Beria regarded Swiatlo's report as so important that he went straight to Stalin himself with it. The marshal was enraged. The remarkable range of Field's contacts throughout the whole of the bloc, his ability to move seemingly at will between Eastern and Western Europe, the way he had insinuated himself into the confidence of so many East and West European Communists should never have been permitted to happen. The warning signs had been there for all to see for years. He had disobeyed a party instruction in the thirties by going to Geneva instead of staying at his post in Washington, clear evidence of where his loyalties lay; it was well known that he had contacts with Allen Dulles, and it was equally well known that he was personally responsible for bringing Communists who had been incurably softened by their contact with the West back to Eastern Europe after the war and establishing them indirectly in positions of authority. Beria, as the Americans knew he would, insisted upon independent checks.

So it was that the CIA's resident double agent (who still cannot be named because of state security reasons) was pressed into service by the Russians. A desk officer working within CIA headquarters in Washington, he was thought by the Russians to be a Communist spy, but, as a junior State Department official in the mid-thirties, he had immediately informed his superiors when he was approached by a Soviet agent. He had been carefully nurtured by the U.S. ever since. On no occasion had he sent deliberately false information to Russia. He was being saved for just such an event as this.

There are only a limited number of occasions when a "double" can be used. An agent who transmits information which subsequently turns out to be false is never fully trusted again. Agent X's track record was perfect; his reports, though never necessarily of high moment, were nevertheless always accurate. His track record was now to be broken.

Within a few days Agent X was able to report to the CIA that he had been asked for information about Noel Field. Back went his reply, carefully guarded and subtly worded. He had not been able to gain access to the Noel Field files, though he could confirm that they existed. Talk in the agency was that Field was involved with Allen Dulles, but no one seemed to know anything about him. Going back over several years, every document which could remotely have concerned Field and his activities had been removed from the files. Most interesting of all, though, he was supposedly under investigation for his activities in the State Department before the war and was known as a Communist activist. Agent X apologized for not being able to be more specific. The report was, however, dynamite. It was convincing because it was not specific. There could be little doubt any more in the Soviets' minds that Field was a U.S. agent.

But another piece of clinching evidence was to come the way of the MVD. Lieutenant General Fedor Belkin, the squat, bull-necked commander-in-chief of the Southeast European division of the MVD, in charge of the Soviet secret police in Hungary, Austria, Germany, Czechoslovakia, Poland, Rumania, Bulgaria and Albania, was chosen by the CIA as the man to deliver the *coup de grâce*. On a visit to the Soviet zone in Vienna, he was contacted by an Englishman named Hathaway, one of his regular informants, who told him that SIS and CIA people were quarreling over the activities of a man called Field who, Hathaway said, was luring SIS operatives into the CIA by offering them more money than the British could afford and thereby damaging the SIS network in Czechoslovakia.*

The Czechs, of course, already had a fairly voluminous file on Noel Field. In October 1948 Field, asking for a

---

* Mention of Czechoslovakia in the approach to Belkin had been a subtle touch, for Czechoslovakia, economically and politically the most advanced of Communist countries, with a tradition of Western-style parliamentary democracy behind her, had been a hunting ground for British intelligence and the Americans for some time. Already, independent of Washington, SIS had started a minor propaganda campaign of its own, a clever counterintelligence ruse which was paying dividends. During the forties, MI5 had become increasingly worried about the presence in Parliament of a great number of left-wing M.P.s who had swept to power in the Labour landslide victory of 1945 and who, in many cases, MI5 believed were of dubious loyalty. The Iron Curtain embassy receptions were packed with M.P.s who were easily flattered by big dinner parties and even more so by all-expenses-paid trips on delegations to countries behind the Iron Curtain. MI5 regarded them as a potential, if not an actual, security hazard, but it was politically defenseless in doing anything about them. Unable to discredit them at home, MI5 proceeded to discredit them abroad in the hope that first, if they passed on information, they would not be believed, and second, that they would eventually be cut off as "hostiles" by their erstwhile hosts. (The effects of this operation are still being felt, which explains why many Communists, especially those who went through the forties and fifties, are easier in the presence of Conservatives than they are with Socialists.) So successful was this, that in August 1948, two Czech security officers (one the head of internal political counterintelligence and the other the head of the security and personnel sections of the security police) wrote to President Gottwald, Prime Minister Zapotocky and Party Secretary Slansky saying that Czechoslovakia was "more than ever a hunting ground for foreign agents. . . . We consider that many British nationals advertising themselves as leftists, or even Communists, are trained agents of the intelligence service. . . . It seems that in the Slav countries, in general, the intelligence service is fond of using ostensible Communists or left intellectuals." It was a description which could have fitted Noel Field exactly. The letter went on with this dire warning: "We point out that such a small staff of intelligence officers cannot safeguard the Republic. We fear that serious attacks on individuals may happen at any moment, we suspect that treason of a most grave nature is already rife, that the most secret documents are known to the enemy or may become known to him at any moment."

Czech resident's permit, with the hope of getting a job as a
lecturer at Charles University in Prague, gave as references several Czech Communists whom he had known and
helped. All of them appear to have been careful enough to
express a measure of doubt about him and, when it became
known that inquiries were being made, others who had met
him immediately volunteered information. It was decided,
though never communicated to Field, that he would not be
given permission to stay in the country. No further action
was planned.

Now things were to be very different. With his "information" about Field, General Belkin flew to Moscow for
consultations with Beria and also for a final pep talk from
Stalin, who had become personally involved in the affair.
Field was not only a spy but unquestionably the spearhead
of an awesome and frightening Anglo-American-Yugoslav
drive to shatter the very fabric of the Communist bloc.
Nothing, Stalin decreed, was as important as destroying
Field and the nest of vipers he controlled. Belkin was given
a free hand to achieve this aim.

In Washington, after developing a neat, protective
wrapping for the operation, Allen Dulles sat back and
waited for the explosion. In order to avoid the dangers of
premature discovery, he leaked the operation himself—but
it was the mirror image he now presented to the outside
world.

His agents let it be known—and his brother, John
Foster Dulles, in what appeared a monumental indiscre-
tion, spoke of it in public—that Operation X had been
mounted by the CIA. Its purpose was to infiltrate American agents into the highest echelons of the Communist
party and governments of Eastern Europe. It was an
extremely clever finishing touch. Any double agents inside

the CIA or SIS* who accidentally came across the operation would assume that it was Operation X. The Russians, knowing of Operation X, would more readily believe evidence that some of their most trusted servants were American spies. So the real operation created fictitious spies. Operation X, a fictitious operation, created real spies —Soviet agents spying on their colleagues. The package was complete.

The operation had an almost poetic quality about it. Dulles had suffered because he had unwittingly smoothed the way for East European Communists to achieve power in their own countries after the war. Now he was creating a situation whereby those same people would find themselves out of jobs and probably inside a prison because of the connection they had had with him. He had been duped by Noel Field; now Noel Field would be destroyed by that association. Every disloyalty Field had committed to the United States had been turned around so that it became a disloyalty to the Soviet Union.

As for the Russians, they would be fed such a conspiracy that they would choke themselves in the eating. A new dark age would descend upon the peoples of Eastern Europe. Truth would become a political liability, the lie an instrument of state policy. Torture and death would be an everyday norm; the prisons would fill with men who had sacrificed their lives for the cause which was now destroying them; the courts would become the playthings of petty

---

* Perhaps one of the best-known double agents of our time is Kim Philby, who joined SIS in 1941 but had been recruited five years previously by the Russians as one of their agents. In 1949 he was posted to Washington as first secretary in the British embassy, but in reality he was a liaison man between the CIA and SIS. In 1951 he managed to tip off two other Russian agents—Guy Burgess and Donald Maclean —that they were about to be arrested, and so they escaped to Russia. In 1963 Philby followed them to Moscow, where he lives today.

tyrants. In the hands of a master like Joseph Stalin nothing, Dulles knew, would be excluded.

It may now seem a cruel fate to have wished upon the
peoples of Eastern Europe. But Dulles had no doubt that
their salvation could lie only in making the journey to hell
and back. They had to know the reality of Stalinism in
order to be forced to fight. That they would eventually rise
and outface the obscene challenge which he himself was
now laying down, he had no doubt. Had not the Russians
themselves only really begun to fight when they experienced the true nature of German savagery? Has any revolution ever flourished under a benevolent dictatorship? So
the lesson had to be learned: man fights for change only
when not to do so is no longer a viable alternative. Dulles's
lesson would drive a wedge between the satellites and
Moscow; the giant monolith would shatter as the parts, one
after the other, crushed by the burden of Stalinism, would
slowly and inexorably splinter.

The plan lacked only one thing: an agency code name.
Dulles thought about it for quite some time and then
scrawled across the top cover of the document file in his
well-known handwriting the legend "Operation Splinter
Factor."

Chapter 7

The Family That Disappeared

On May 5, 1949, Noel Field boarded Air France Flight Number 240 at Paris Le Bourget, en route for Prague and a future which again seemed to hold some promise. Exhilarated by the prospects of a challenging job, happy that any misunderstanding between him and the Russians seemed to have been cleared away, Noel kissed Herta goodbye at the airport and passed through immigration control.

Perhaps if he hadn't been quite so desperate he would have thought it odd that the suggestion that he come to Czechoslovakia to be considered for a post as a lecturer at Prague's world-famous Charles University had been made over the telephone rather than by letter. Equally, he might have been surprised by the ease with which he got his visa. The Czech embassy in Paris knew all about him and stamped his passport in record time. An alert man would, perhaps, have stopped there and then. But Noel Field failed to detect a single false note.

Friends to whom he made his farewells in Paris couldn't remember the last time they had seen him looking so happy or so well. All the old effervescence, bottled up by months of fear and frustration, bubbled out again. He had plans once again, an option on the future, and that was a marvelous feeling.

Herta left Paris as well (both had been attending the Partisans for Peace Congress) in order to pack the family possessions in Geneva so that she could join him in Prague as soon as he had settled in. She heard from him on May 8 by telephone when he urged her to come quickly because he was looking for an apartment, principally because hotel and restaurant food was proving too heavy for a stomach which had always given him trouble. On May 10, coincidentally, both the Fields, Noel from Prague and Herta from Geneva, wrote optimistically about the way things were working out to Noel's sister, Elsie, in the United States.

A day later, on May 11, two men called for Field at the Palace Hotel, a dingy mausoleum of a place which had seen better days. The three of them left the hotel a little later, Field apparently unconcerned and unruffled and, according to the hotel manager, walking in the direction of Wenceslas Square, the center of Prague.

A few days later a friend called the Palace and was told that Field was understood to be on a short trip to Hungary but his room was still being paid for. Forty-eight hours later the manager received a telegram from Field, from Bratislava, on the Czech-Hungarian border, saying he wished to vacate his room and that a René Kimmel would be arriving to pick up his luggage. Mr. Kimmel, according to the manager, duly turned up and took possession of Noel Field's few effects. Then there was silence.

For two months Herta Field kept quiet. Somehow, she felt, if she didn't make a fuss, Noel would reemerge. Neither the American embassy nor any official source was asked for assistance. By July she could bear it no longer and flew to Paris to meet Noel's younger brother, Hermann, who was on his way to an architects' congress in Italy. She told him that she intended to fly to Prague and try to find out what had happened. Hermann agreed to help and promised to join her in Prague as soon as the meeting was over.

They used the Palace Hotel in Prague as their headquarters, making the rounds of the city, vainly seeking information. At the ministries they met blank incomprehension and discouragement. People promised to make inquiries but always came back with the same answer: there was no trace of Noel.

Hermann had to go on to Warsaw and promised Herta that he'd make some inquiries there and then return to Prague for a day before flying back to America via London, where he'd left his English wife, Kate, and their two children. On August 22 friends drove him to Warsaw's Okecie Airport for the two-hour flight back to Prague. They watched him file through passport control and immigration and waved a final goodbye as he turned to them before disappearing into the final departure lounge. When the plane reached Prague, Hermann Field was not aboard. Nor, as a by now totally distraught Herta discovered, was his name even on the passenger list.

When Kate Field, Hermann's wife, went to London Airport to meet her husband in from Prague and discovered that not only was he not on the flight but had not previously canceled his reservation, she did what perhaps

should have been done months before: she went to the
American embassy in Grosvenor Square and reported that
Hermann and Noel were missing behind the Iron Curtain.

Coincidentally, Herta had also at last decided that the
American embassy was the only hope left to her. So on
August 25 she reported there. The embassy promised to
make inquiries on her behalf. On August 26 the embassy
telephoned Herta at the Palace Hotel. They were told that
she had checked out. Herta Field had disappeared.

Just over a year later, a beautiful twenty-eight-year-
old German girl, Erica Glaser Wallach, who had been
looked after throughout the war by Noel and Herta Field
and was regarded by the press as his adopted daughter and
by Noel himself as "my little girl," crossed from West Germany into East Berlin to see if she could track down Noel,
Hermann and Herta. It seemed, by any standards, a for-
lorn hope, but Erica Wallach was no ordinary girl.

Erica Glaser was born in Schlawe, Pomerania, in the
northeastern corner of Germany on February 19, 1922. Her
father was a doctor, half Jewish, and an active anti-Nazi.
Her brother, three years older than she, refused to join the
Hitler Youth and was forced to move to England to complete his education. After joining the British army, he rose
to the rank of captain and was subsequently killed on
active service in 1945.

In December 1935 her father and mother fled Germany, taking thirteen-year-old Erica to Spain, where her
father, because he spoke the language and also had a Spanish license to practice medicine, began a new life. During
the Spanish civil war Dr. Glaser, politically left-wing as he
was, worked as a physician for the Loyalist army until his
medical team was transferred to the Communist International Brigade, where he served as a captain until the end
of the war in 1939. Erica, who was only fourteen when the

war broke out, and her mother worked as nurses in an International Brigade hospital.

Dr. Glaser, in fact, was not a Communist and got into trouble for his non-Communist views. As Erica later testified to a Congressional committee:

> As a matter of fact, he had many difficulties in Spain . . . because he was not a Communist and because he could never close his mouth: he said what he thought. And three times, he was kicked out of hospital, as head of the hospital, for political reasons. Once he was to be shot, for being an anti-Communist and, you know, all sorts of accusations, espionage against the Left and so on and so forth. . . .

When the war came to a close in 1939, the position of the Glasers was terrible indeed. Erica, now seventeen, was suffering from typhoid fever and had to be evacuated to the French border. Unexpectedly, someone called on her and told her that an American couple, Herta and Noel Field, who knew her parents from visiting their hospital in Spain, wished to "adopt" her and take her to the United States.

Surprised and mystified by the offer, Erica went to see her parents. This is how she described the scene:

> It was the most dreadful place I have ever seen. You know, big camp—people were lying in the streets, in the mud, wounded. . . . I finally found my mother in a theater. There was a little theater in that village, and on the stage in bed . . . was my mother half dead.

Erica was separated from her parents again by World War II and throughout those six years was looked after by the Fields. She was the child they never had.

Since Erica had been a victim of fascism herself and was now being cared for by a man who was both an ideological communist and, as she could see, a man doing a great deal of good for thousands of people, it is only natural that she looked upon communism as being some kind of answer to the problems of a world which had so blindly struck out at herself and so many others.

Because she spoke German and was a member of the Field household, she came into contact with leading German Communists who were waiting out the war as refugees in Switzerland. Because of these contacts, she unwittingly became a part of the Field operation, designed to smuggle Communists into the occupied territories—mainly Germans back into Germany, many of whom, to Allen Dulles's subsequent chagrin, eventually took top positions inside the East German Communist party. But Dulles had a personal ax to grind with her too.

Since Dulles still believed at the end of the war that Noel Field was a respectable patriot, she got a job as a secretary to a member of Dulles's staff, an OSS operative called Gerhard P. van Arkel, and went with him from Switzerland to the OSS headquarters in Wiesbaden in Germany. Later, she went with van Arkel to Berlin, where he worked with the German labor movement while she wore a U.S. Army uniform and lived in OSS headquarters.

Erica made it plain to the German Communists that she was prepared to spy upon the American for whom she worked, but, by one of those incredible pieces of bureaucratic bungling which characterizes Communist party branches so frequently, she was told that she would have to quit the OSS before she became a party member. So Erica left the OSS and became, in turn, secretary of the Communist party of the Hesse parliament, and in January 1947 her name appeared on the masthead as editor of *Wissen und Tat,* a German Communist party magazine.

To Dulles, who had used her a great deal in Switzerland and who was now clearly entitled to believe that she had been an active Communist agent, this public admission of her Communist faith was to him a direct and personally aimed slap in the face—indeed, the final humiliating blow in the Field saga as it unfolded after the war.

Erica, in fact, was far too independent to fit snugly into the straitjacket imposed by a Communist party organization and was quickly quarreling with her masters. To make matters worse, she fell in love with and decided to marry a young U.S. Army captain, Bob Wallach, and in 1948 wrote the Central Committee in Germany resigning her membership.

Because of her Communist affiliations and no doubt Dulles's ire, Erica was denied permission to enter the United States, despite the fact that Bob was a GI and an American citizen. He found it impossible even to get work with an American organization in Europe because of his wife's politics, so under the GI Bill of Rights he enrolled as a student in the Sorbonne.

In the spring of 1950 Erica decided it was time to do something about Noel and Herta, whom she loved and to whom she felt a deep debt of gratitude. She contacted her old friend Leo Bauer (now a member of the Politburo) in East Berlin and asked if he could go to Frankfurt to meet her. Soon a letter came from Bauer suggesting it was "very important" that they meet, but that he couldn't go to Frankfurt.

Erica immediately went to the American consulate in Geneva, saying she was going to Berlin to try to obtain information about Noel. The consulate agreed with the plan and suggested that since it was important to find out details about what had happened to the family, the American embassy would be prepared to pay her fares and expenses. She refused this on the basis that to accept would

mark her as an American agent and make her vulnerable.
So she decided to move without letting the consulate know
her travel plans.

But the CIA was one jump ahead of her all the way.
For she too had been marked down by the Splinter Factor
operatives as someone to be presented to the Communists
as a top American agent. She tried to telephone Bauer
from West Berlin, but was told by his secretary that he
was out. She called another friend, a woman, also in the
higher echelons of the party, who told her that she did not
know Bauer's address and that it could be obtained only
by going to the Communist party headquarters in the
Eastern section.

And so she locked her money and documents in the
cupboard in her hotel room and simply took the subway to
the wrong side of the Iron Curtain. At party headquarters
the doormen knew nothing of Bauer but mentioned a
Communist party congress taking place in the city. She
went there hoping that he might be one of the delegates.
Eventually, she met someone who seemed to know Bauer
and who said that he had gone to Thuringia to get his wife,
who was ill, and he would probably return in the morning
to Berlin. As she left the building, she thought:

> My God, I made it. I'm going to get back to the hotel
> and . . . write a card to Bob . . . that unfortunately it
> didn't work and I will have to stay until Monday. I was
> just figuring that out in my mind when I heard steps
> behind me, and I knew that was the end. I didn't turn
> around. And after a second, somebody just put a hand
> on my shoulder and said, "Criminal Police. Would you
> please come around the corner with us."

An entire family had simply walked into oblivion.
Operation Splinter Factor had claimed the Fields.

Chapter 8

For Peter From Wagner

As far as Washington was concerned, what happened to the Fields was unimportant. They were merely to be the means to an end. They would be used to provide the evidence which would finally discredit some of the great men of Eastern Europe—Wladyslaw Gomulka of Poland, party first secretary, Laszlo Rajk of Hungary, minister of the interior, Traicho Kostov of Bulgaria, deputy prime minister, and many others. All were Communists, hard and uncompromising, yet all believed that Russia should be their ally, not their master. They believed that trade negotiations between them and the Russians should be genuine negotiations, not a blind acceptance of Soviet demands. They felt they should be allowed to trade with the West to help rebuild their shattered economies. Although they pledged their support to the principles of Marxism-Leninism, they

wanted to adapt communism to the particular needs of
their countries and peoples as they emerged from the war.
They were prepared to be allies of Moscow—even more
than that—but not colonies. At best they were patriots; at
worst they believed that they could not survive politically
if unadulterated Stalinism was permitted to dictate the
course of their countries' futures.

It was precisely for that reason that Allen Dulles and
his colleagues were now laying the trap which would
destroy them. Their brand of communism—which, for
example, in the case of Poland still permitted the peasants
to own land—had certain attractions for the lower class
and was defensible to the intellectuals. Only the middle
class and the old aristocracy would find it objectionable;
but the former would either flee or come to accept it, and
the latter had long since been totally discredited as a political force. It was Dulles's object to give them a platform, to
show communism to be the evil that he thought it was.
Nationalist Communists were making communism acceptable to the people, and so, accordingly, they had to be
removed.

The first step had been taken. The men who were
eventually to implicate these nationalist Communists had
been arrested. Noel Field had been, in fact, picked up by
the Hungarians. Lieutenant General Belkin had decreed
that Hungary was the center of the conspiracy, which was
an attempt to rend Eastern Europe out of the embraces of
the Soviet Union. Stalin had agreed with Belkin's analysis.
Certainly there seemed to be in Hungary, supplying as it
had the entire Rakosi Division in the Spanish civil war, an
army of people who had known Noel Field. They had
worked with him and Yugoslav Communists during the
war, and, in subsequent negotiations with Moscow after
the war, seemed to be pushing the Hungarian road to

socialism with a vigor which made them suspect from the earliest days.

Matyas Rakosi, the unpleasant and vicious first secretary of the Hungarian Communist party and chairman of the Council of Ministers, on the orders of Stalin himself, had asked the Czechs to arrange the arrest of Noel Field. Initially, the Czechs resisted. Rakosi linked Field with a prominent prewar Communist lawyer, Dr. Gejza Pavlik (then director of Cedok, the Czechoslovak travel bureau), who was liked and respected by the Czech party leadership. He was known as a good friend of Noel Field's, and was responsible for doling out Unitarian Services Committee assistance in Czechoslovakia after the war, a provision of which was that he send occasional reports on social and economic conditions in the areas needing help. But he had cleared this with the party, which had agreed that he should go ahead. Moreover, the party was not particularly impressed with the evidence against Noel Field. Their own investigations months earlier had suggested that if he was an American agent, he was not an especially dangerous one; it was certainly not worth harming the international prestige of Czechoslovakia by inveigling him to Prague in order to arrest him.

But the Splinter Factor conspiracy was considerably bigger than men like Jindrich Vesely, head of the Czech security services, who initially rejected the Hungarian demand. Belkin, on hearing of Vesely's reluctance to act, flew to Prague and put his demands in person to President Gottwald himself. Abusive and threatening, he insisted that the president take the Hungarian request seriously. When asked politely why Hungary did not do its own dirty work, Belkin replied patiently that Noel Field could never be persuaded to go to a country which was at the very heart of the plot he was stage-managing. But he trusted the Czechs. Gottwald eventually agreed and told Vesely: "If General Belkin, too, has verified it and supports it, then do as they [the Hungarians] want."

So Field was lured to Czechoslovakia by the promise of a job at Charles University. The moment he arrived he was kept under around-the-clock surveillance until the two senior Hungarian secret policemen could be flown in to make the arrest. He was taken back to Budapest and immediately subjected to a vicious day-and-night interrogation directed by the feared head of the Hungarian secret police, Gabor Peter.

As for Hermann Field, when he arrived in Poland a message went to Stalin asking whether he too should be arrested. The reply came back in the affirmative. But in the best traditions of counterespionage, Hermann was permitted to remain at liberty for as long as he was meeting Poles who could lead the security services to the heart of the conspiracy. The decision to arrest him as he was boarding the plane taking him out of the country was made by Lieutenant Colonel Swiatlo, and it was Swiatlo himself who was waiting in the final departure lounge of the airport and who invited him to an adjoining room, informed him he was wanted for questioning and drove him off to a prison cell. Efforts were made to break him too, but he was never considered as dangerous as his brother, and indeed Noel's interrogation was already paying fantastic dividends.

Noel admitted to his contacts with Allen Dulles during the war and also to having introduced many senior Communists to Dulles, who had helped them and their organizations with money, often very large sums; he admitted that Yugoslav Communists had been prominent in all of the camps he ran and that though Hungarians tended to stick with Hungarians and Czechs with Czechs, the Yugoslavs, probably because their resistance was as active as it was, knew no national boundaries in the friends and contacts they made. He admitted that many Hungarians, with his help, had crossed back into Hungary through Yugoslavia with the active help of Tito's partisans; he admitted to being an intermediary between Tito and the Americans; he admitted that the other Communist groups in Switzerland looked upon the Yugoslavs with respect and even affection. For all this, of course, he had an explanation, but he had come up against something so great that nothing could be explained away. He was dealing with a man in the advanced stages of paranoia, being tormented by psychologists of genius—the American masterminds of the plot.

Believe that Noel Field was a well-meaning, misguided, slightly inept American fellow traveler, and all of his actions during the war could be explained away and understood. Believe from the beginning, however, that he was an American agent of a great seniority, and everything he ever did could be seen as a confirmation of the double life he was supposed to have led. In the hands of skilled interrogators, he never stood a chance.

He claimed that he was a dedicated Communist; then why did he deal for years with the man every government in Eastern Europe knew was the most dangerous enemy of them all, Allen Dulles? He claimed that his Communist friends were motivated by only one consideration and that was to destroy the Fascists; then why did they take money from arch-Fascist Dulles? He claimed that his and his associates' friendships with the Yugoslavs were, in the circumstances of war, innocent; then why during all those years had they not suspected the Titoist conspiracy which so obviously had been brewing all that time?

He denied that the Unitarian Services Committee was

a cover for American espionage; then how was it that the
man who recruited him, Robert Dexter, was known to be a
full-time member of the OSS? For was it not Dexter who
had suggested that Field and his friends cooperate with
Dulles?

Was it really to be believed that in time of war, in
Vichy France, the OSS had failed to grasp an opportunity
of putting a man with a perfect cover into Marseilles? Was
it possible that, having infiltrated its man Dexter into the
Unitarian organization as head of the entire European
committee, the OSS had not seen to it that his successor,
Noel Field, was also a senior member of the American wartime secret service, especially stationed as he was in such
an important area as Switzerland?

So tight was the trap, so neatly conceived the operation, that even those acts in which Field had betrayed his
duty to his Unitarian sponsors on behalf of the Communists were now used against him with crushing effect. Why
had he excluded non-Communists from his camps? To help
party members? But surely he had earlier claimed there
was a humanitarian need above politics, and who could
deny that this was so? Was not his interest in Communists
both unhealthy and unsupportable? Was it not more likely
that the OSS would use this method of helping Communists so as to put them forever in its debt, to be able to
suborn them and blackmail them in the future?

Was it pure coincidence that he had chosen the Communists on the Dulles list to help return to Eastern
Europe? Was he really expecting his interrogators to
believe that Dulles would willingly help people whom he
knew to be his enemy? Or did Dulles, with Field's help,
send back only those people who were by then already in
the pay of American intelligence?

After a fortnight, Field confessed to being an American agent, but, finding strength from somewhere, he went back on his confession the following day, never to repeat it.

But General Belkin was unconcerned. As the reports of the interrogation flowed from the prison cell daily, there was no doubt in his mind, or Stalin's, that Field was indeed what they believed him to be, an American agent who had corrupted or was about to corrupt the entire party throughout the Soviet bloc. Actually, in view of the story which Field told voluntarily, it was easier for Stalin to believe that this was the case than that it was not. Indeed, even today, the real story leaves a twinge of doubt; how so many people could be quite so stupid beggars the imagination. Given the political atmosphere then, his guilt could hardly ever have been in question. To Stalin, however, Noel Field was only interesting insofar as the people he contacted were interesting. If he were merely an American spy, then he would have been shot or exchanged for a Soviet agent at some opportune moment. But Field, Stalin was persuaded, was more than that: he was the center of a conspiracy, the spider in a massive web which was choking the life out of his dominions.

Meanwhile, throughout Eastern Europe, that enormous army of people unfortunate enough to have known Noel or Hermann Field were picked up and questioned. Few were initially, at least, of any importance; they were, by and large, members of the International Brigade which had fought so fiercely in Spain against Franco. Noel Field had known nearly all of them, had helped and succored them when, the war lost, they were left to rot in French internment camps. Many of them, having endured that, went on to fight the Nazis in national resistance movements, were caught, tortured, put into concentration camps and emerged from the war with their health broken but their faith in communism strengthened, if anything, by their hideous experiences. Noel Field was able to help again, with clinics and medical facilities to assist their recovery. Then, either through the OSS and Allen Dulles or some other way, he got them back to their own countries to help usher in the "new dawn."

These people were, in every sense, the best of the breed—men and women who had been prepared to sacrifice comfort, career, health and their lives for a cause whose demands were always written in ultimatums but for which they gladly gave all they had. They were now entitled to expect that, with the destruction of the old bourgeois parties and the climb to power of Communist governments, they, the champions of that victory, would be entitled to bask, for the first time in their lives, in the luxury of political security. No more, provided they kept the civil laws of the country, would they be imprisoned, tortured or starved; no more would they be the outcasts of society; no more would they have to sacrifice every bodily comfort in order to belong to an illegal organization, harried and persecuted at every turn.

But it was not to work out that way. The moment they were connected in any way with either of the Field brothers, they were condemned. It is not difficult to understand the despair and fear they must have felt, realizing that the torture they once experienced and miraculously survived would again be inflicted upon them. Many committed suicide. Some panicked—they knew they could not survive a second time around—and in Hungary, Poland and Czechoslovakia made vain and inept attempts to contact American or British escape organizations. Known by now as the Fieldists, members of an international conspiracy with its headquarters in Washington and Belgrade, they managed only to dig the pit deeper for themselves and their fellows. They were already doomed, for Comrade Stalin knew them all.

The little people were the first to suffer. In Poland, Anna Duracz, Berman's loyal secretary, was arrested almost immediately. Ironically, Berman himself survived the investigation and was later able to provide his own version of what had happened:

> In the case of Anna Duracz, there was direct interven-
> tion on Stalin's part. I was against the arrest until the
> very end. I am, was, deeply convinced of her innocence,
> not knowing at the time how much truth there was in
> the charges made against Field. Comrade Bierut
> defended me from the slanderous charges of espionage
> for a number of years; he did it with complete dedication
> and self-sacrifice, and the accusations were always
> renewed. . . . We know very well what the fate was of
> those who, in 1949, and in the years after, were under
> the charge of having been in contact with Field. There is
> no doubt that had Comrade Bierut not defended my case
> so well, I could, at the most, be exhumed today.

This statement before the Central Committee of the Polish Communist party in 1956 by the man who, without knowing it, was at the very heart of the matter is a remarkable testimony to the tragedy which slowly began to unfold.

So intense was his personal interest in the Field conspiracy that Joseph Stalin had taken time off from onerous affairs of state to insist upon the imprisonment and interrogation of a mere secretary to a top party official in Poland.

It didn't take General Belkin long to discover the main conspirators. The Czech records show that on May 28, after Noel Field's arrest, a Colonel Szucs, a senior officer within Hungarian security, arrived in Prague requesting the arrest of Gejza Pavlik. Tibor Szonyi, head of the Cadre Department of the Hungarian Central Committee and thus responsible for all governmental and party appointments throughout the country, had been arrested and had also provided evidence linking Pavlik with the Fieldist conspiracy. Szonyi's arrest was the first indication of how high General Belkin was reaching, for Szonyi's job—as a kind of personnel officer for the nation—put him high up in the leadership. But Szonyi was a natural. Like Noel Field, all of his actions in 1944 and 1945, which may have appeared perfectly natural and even praiseworthy then, took on a very different hue a few years later.

To the Russians, who now believed in the Fieldist conspiracy, there was no doubt that Szonyi was a spy. He had led the large Hungarian Communist contingent in Switzerland during the war. He had taken money from Noel Field to assist his group and had even given a receipt for it. In 1945 he was assisted back into Hungary with forged papers, provided by a Yugoslav member of the OSS, which showed him to be a Yugoslav officer; four thousand Swiss francs to help him and his group with expenses were supplied by Dulles via Noel Field; and finally and most damning of all, there was his letter to the OSS office in Belgrade, indicating a trust between him and the American agency, in which he requested assistance to get through to Hungary.

But Szonyi was not the target either—his task was to point the way. The moment he was arrested, there was never any question that Szonyi would implicate his friend and mentor Laszlo Rajk, one of the best-known Communist leaders of Eastern Europe, first Communist minister of the interior after the war, later foreign minister and the only real rival in the party to Matyas Rakosi.

Handsome, only forty years old, a first-class orator with a mind to match, a wit and *bon viveur*, Laszlo Rajk had a genuine personal popularity among the people, which permitted him, like so few of his colleagues, to mix with

ordinary Hungarians with ease and friendliness. He was
finely attuned to the temper of the times and could be
uncomfortably ruthless when it suited him. His period as
minister of the interior was marked by the systematic
destruction of non-Communist parties in Hungary, political trials and killings.

If Rajk maintained the orthodox and rather frightening creed of Communist revolutionaries—that capitalism
was a form of applied violence against the working classes
and that it could be eradicated only by violent methods—
he was not alone in that belief or even, if one accepts
communism as the ultimate truth, necessarily wrong. He
himself had suffered at the hands of the police during Hungary's prewar Fascist regime, was imprisoned several times
and severely beaten. From a poor family of shoemakers,
and a Communist from student days, he had been an
active underground fighter in an illegal party and was
known both for his intellectual ability and his personal
courage.

He led the Rakosi battalion in the Spanish civil war
and ended up in a French internment camp, where he had
the misfortune, as it subsequently turned out, to meet
briefly and talk to Noel Field. By 1942 he had arranged his
return to Hungary, with Yugoslav Communist assistance,
and became one of the most prominent men in the anti-
Nazi, anti-Fascist underground.

In the postwar reconstructed Communist-front government, Rajk was soon marked out as one of the most
important and able Communists in the land and, as a
result, among non-Communists, became feared and hated.
They saw in his fanatical faith a greater danger than the
more cynical approach of his colleagues. They felt his whip-
lash and knew him to be incorruptible. Equally they
knew the mood of the people: if he ever took over from the

slimy Rakosi, then, because he had a measure of popularity himself, communism would become more acceptable to the people of the nation.

But Rajk was feared and mistrusted by his colleagues. Unlike the more senior men in the government and party, his political education had little to do with Moscow. Yet oddly enough, he probably trusted the Russians and accepted their good intentions a good deal more than did his Moscow-trained fellow ministers. They had seen the practice of Stalinism firsthand, had lost that idealistic faith which so many had about the wonders of the Soviet Union and which to an extent Rajk still maintained. Neither did Soviet power disturb him unduly. Hungary had, after all, entered the war on the side of the Nazis with a Fascist government at its head. The remnants of that regime were still very much alive and kicking, and without the Red Army to help them, Hungarian Communists would have been dangerously alone. Yet Rajk also maintained that this was a temporary state of affairs and was not prepared to concede that Moscow should always give the orders. Cooperation between Hungary and Russia was essential for the well-being of the state, but it had to be a willing cooperation of mutual respect brought about because the political and economic interests of each of the two countries happened to coincide. He suspected that Matyas Rakosi would sell out Hungarian interests to the Soviets whenever they demanded it, and he made his feelings known.

In July 1948 Rajk was appointed foreign minister. Immediately the assumption was made—and it is still current among serious historians—that this was the first step in his eventual slide from power. This was not the case. Rajk had won a political victory, however temporary, over his colleagues. Even Rakosi told his intimates: "At last, the Foreign Office won't have a kindergarten teacher at its head." Rajk, it was believed, and he clearly thought so

himself, was strong enough to face up to the Russians with
whom, as foreign minister, he would deal; he would be
tough enough to be able to insist upon the ultimate sovereignty of the Hungarian government and people. His
appointment as foreign minister was an unpopular one as
far as the Russians were concerned, and Stalin himself
managed to convince Rakosi that all he had achieved was
to set up a powerful rival.

At the same time, the CIA was busy trying to discredit Laszlo Rajk. The campaign to destroy him in the
eyes of Stalin and Rakosi began in 1948. He was presented
to Western journalists by the State Department, the Quai
d'Orsay and the Foreign Office in London as a Hungarian
national who disagreed strongly with the Sovietization of
his country. Stories of alleged rows between him and Rakosi—most of them inaccurate—flowed thick and fast in the
Western press. His appointment as foreign minister was
described as a serious fall from grace as a result of his
nationalistic policies.

Meanwhile, his mailbag swelled with letters from
Hungarian nationals abroad who knew him in his student
days, in Spain or in the internment camps, or who alleged
they knew him. They all bore common characteristics:
they congratulated him on his government posts, they
thanked him for being a true Hungarian patriot and they
recalled some private statement of his, from earlier years,
which, when analyzed, revealed a massive Trotskyist
deviation. There was another similarity too: they were all
written by the same man, today a professor at Georgetown
University in Washington, who, between 1947 and 1949, on
the directions of the CIA, did little else but compose poi-
son-pen letters in others' names to prominent personalities
behind the Iron Curtain for the secret police to open and
dissect. At about the same time, messages "for Peter from
Wagner" were intercepted by the security. The belief was

that "Wagner" was both Allen Dulles and Noel Field, and "Peter," Szonyi. Rajk was mentioned as a contact in at least one.

Within three weeks of Noel Field's arrest and a week of Szonyi's, Laszlo Rajk was a condemned man. Evidence extracted from these two, and the evidence of others, indicated that a major conspiracy existed, that the Yugoslavs were at the heart of it and that Rajk was Tito's henchman in Hungary. Rajk had done one very foolish thing. In October 1948, after he had become foreign minister, he agreed to meet Tito's minister of the interior, Aleksandar Rankovitch, secretly, in an old hunting lodge on the Hungarian side of the Hungarian-Yugoslavian border. In these talks Rajk sought to persuade the Yugoslavs to moderate their attitudes toward Moscow. He sympathized with their stand but believed that by making such a public issue of it, the Yugoslavs were playing into the hands of the Americans. Rankovitch asked the Hungarians to stand up for Yugoslavia in the Cominform. The meeting was one between ministers of two neighboring countries in dispute with each other and seeking a way out of the impasse. In normal times, this initiative would have been perfectly natural, but these were not normal times and Rajk should have known it. The meeting was a remarkable error of judgment, a display of political arrogance, for which he would never be forgiven.*

Later in 1948 Rajk, in fact, was called to Moscow (his only visit to the cradle of the Revolution), where he was reminded where his duty lay. But the Russians on that

---

* Negotiating with a government whose head, Marshal Tito, was being described on Moscow radio and in the Russian press by such epithets as "greedy ape," "insolent dwarf," "chattering parrot," "traitor," "bandit" and "scoundrel," "whose face is a mask disguising the malicious, cunning egoistic soul of a skillful sneak" was more than an error of judgment; it was an act of total irresponsibility. Rajk clearly had not learned from his own period as minister of the interior quite how ruthless the Russians could be with those they believed were working against them behind their backs.

occasion were friendly—young and impetuous he might
have been, but a traitor he was not.

On the evening of June 3, 1949, Laszlo Rajk knew that
that attitude had changed. He was at home watching his
wife, Julia, feeding their five-week-old son when there was
a ring at the door and his mother-in-law went to see who it
was. At her bidding, he went into the hall to find four
members of the AVH, the Hungarian political police. They
told him that their chief, Gabor Peter, wanted to see him
immediately. Rajk began to protest: if Peter wanted to see
him, he should either come around himself or wait until
the morning. The AVH officers didn't bother to argue.
They seized him, dragged him outside and into a big black
Buick waiting by the curb, thrusting him inside feet first.
That was the last his wife was ever to see of him.

The Buick drew up outside 60, Andrassy Street, the
headquarters of the political police. Still protesting vehe-
mently, he was hauled roughly into the ornately furnished
office of the notorious Gabor Peter. Peter, with no prelimi-
naries, harshly demanded whether he would confess to
being a traitor and a Yugoslav agent. Rajk demanded to
see Matyas Rakosi.

He was struck savagely across the face: "The party's
first secretary," he was told, "does not speak to traitors."
Once again he was dragged away and driven at a furious
pace to one of the large villas which the AVH had expro-
priated on the outskirts of Budapest.

A fellow prisoner, a friend from university days, who
had been arrested a few days previously as a Fieldist, has
written a moving account of how he was confronted by
Rajk in prison seventy-two hours after Rajk's arrest:

> Standing there at the foot of the T-shaped table, staring
> at my former university colleague, I gave not a thought
> to our grotesque situation nor to what lay in store for us.

My attention was concentrated on the three horizontal furrows that disfigured him. When Gabor Peter shouted my name, I turned my eyes away from Rajk's face and looked at Peter. Stressing every word, the head of the Secret Police now asked me: "Who recruited Laszlo Rajk for the party and who established contact between him and the young worker's movement?"

"Istvan Stolte," I replied. . . .

Rajk's eyes strayed across the room. . . .

"Laszlo Rajk: do you admit it?"

Rajk flung the pencil he held in his right hand on to the blank sheets of paper lying on the table and said in a low voice:

"I maintain that it was Messzaros."*

The line of questioning after all these years is of little importance. A party member in the thirties, Istvan Stolte had been expelled for Trotskyist activities and had sought to establish with Trotsky's son, Sedov, a Trotskyist party cell in Hungary. Messzaros was an orthodox Communist. Seeking to connect Rajk with Stolte was merely one strand in the complex web of guilt which would be used to ensnare him. What is important is that the man who had already suffered Gabor Peter's specialty, a soling—the beating of the bare soles of the feet with a rubber truncheon until the feet become swollen to grotesque proportions—was still the foreign minister of his country.

The minutes of the meetings of the Hungarian Council of Ministers on June 8 show that a bill of law was presented in the name of Comrade Rajk. By that time Comrade Rajk had already been in prison for a week. Neither the law nor anything else could help him.

* Bela Szasz, *Volunteers for the Gallows* (London: Chatto & Windus, 1970), p. 37.

Chapter 9

The People's Court in Session

And so the scene was set for the great Communist show trials of the forties and early fifties—trials which were to horrify the world with their brutality and create a schism inside Eastern Europe which time has not yet healed.

The trials were to put the whole of the Communist bloc into a state of nervous shock, reduce all political discussion to the mere making of slogans, and destroy, for the time being at least, the already frail hopes of millions. They created the very conditions Allen Dulles predicted when he first postulated the philosophy behind Operation Splinter Factor.

For, in a very short time, Stalin finally would be robbed of the last vestiges of benevolent paternalism with which he emerged from the war, leaving his successors with the memory of a hated tyrant and the problem of how to maintain an alliance among hostile populations which look back on their immediate past with shame and their immediate future with foreboding.

The trial of "Laszlo Rajk and his accomplices" opened on Friday, September 16, 1949, in the sparsely furnished assembly hall of the headquarters of the Metal and Engineering Workers' Trade Union in Budapest. The proceedings were quiet and matter-of-fact, almost stately. No one would have thought the eight defendants were fighting for their lives. As a matter of fact, they *weren't* fighting. Never once did their defense counsels intervene on their behalf, except at the end to make wishy-washy speeches on mitigation which were nearly as tough as the prosecutor's closing remarks. It wasn't a trial; it was a lynching. The people's court consisted of a judge, Dr. Peter Janko; a journalist, representing the intellectual voice of the country; a "working peasant," representing the land; and a factory worker and a leather worker, representing unskilled and skilled labor respectively. In the distinguished visitors' gallery sat a representative from the people's republic of Poland. Lieutenant Colonel Jozef Swiatlo had begun the process eighteen months before, and now, as a reward, he was permitted to observe the final act of the drama he had helped produce.

It was the moment when all the pieces fell into place, when Operation Splinter Factor became, in terms of political intelligence, pure poetry. For many months, Allen Dulles in Washington had been playing out a complex skein of strings, like a master magician whose hands move so quickly that they dazzle the eye. Suddenly the strings unraveled themselves from their untidy knot, and met there, in public, before the press of the world, in a moment of utter perfection. And even then no one saw the trick.

For the American agent—Dulles's man, Swiatlo—was on the VIP benches of the court of this people's democracy; the loyal Communist and patriot was in the dock on a charge of high treason.

There had been a similar occasion two months previously, when Colonel Swiatlo had gone to Budapest to interrogate, at length, Noel Field, who, having already implicated a great many Hungarian Communists, was now asked for the names of Poles with whom he was acquainted. It was a moment of the purest irony—the American agent, who persuades a Russian spy, in a Hungarian prison, to play the part of stool pigeon on good Polish Communists. Operation Splinter Factor was turning the world upside down.

But now the people's court was in session. The eight Hungarian defendants were Laszlo Rajk, foreign minister; Lieutenant General Gyorgy Palffy, deputy defense minister and army chief of staff; Lazar Brankov, formerly Yugoslav chargé d'affaires in Hungary, who defected to the Hungarians after the Cominform split with Tito; Tibor Szonyi, central personnel secretary; Andras Szalai, Szonyi's deputy; Colonel Bela Korondy of the secret police; Paul Justus, vice-president of the Hungarian radio; and Milan Ogyenovics, a party official.

The indictment read that "Laszlo Rajk and his accomplices initiated and led an organization, the object of which was the overthrow by violence of the democratic state order." All the defendants pleaded guilty and the trial was under way.

Rajk, who had been imprisoned for the past four months, was the first to take the stand. He launched into the most incredible confession of his long catalog of crimes. In 1931, he said, as a young Communist, he was arrested by the police and freed on condition that he spy for the

authorities from within the Communist party. He managed
to smash a strike of building workers by calling a public
meeting, giving the police the opportunity to round up the
ringleaders. He fought in the Spanish civil war, but, in
fact, he deliberately set out to sabotage the Rakosi Division. "To avoid suspicion," he said, "I was sometimes
arrested with the people I had denounced." From Spain he
escaped to a French internment camp, where he made his
first contact with Yugoslav Communists who, even then,
"had Trotskyist tendencies." Then came the first public
mention of Noel Field since he had disappeared four
months previously:

> It was in the Vernet internment camp that an American
> citizen called Field, who was, as far as I know, the head
> of the American intelligence agency for Central and
> Eastern Europe, visited me. . . . He . . . told me that he
> would like to send me home because, as an agent who
> had not been exposed, I would, working in the party,
> according to the instructions received from the Ameri-
> cans, disorganize and dissolve the party and possibly
> even get the party leadership into my hands.

Later, Rajk described how he worked for the Gestapo
during the war and subsequently became a spy for Tito
after being blackmailed by the Yugoslavs, who knew about
his previous activities. He spoke in a cool, dry manner, as if
he were speaking from a narrative he had learned by heart
—which indeed he had.

It was a remarkable performance by any standards;
each word, each gesture had been taught. When the judge
got his lines wrong, Rajk asked him kindly not to interrupt
or he would spoil the flow. Never once did he add a line in
his own defense.

The evidence of the other defendants was at least as

supine as Rajk's. Szonyi's testimony, which, it must be remembered, was prepared for him long before he went into court, indicated how Allen Dulles had skillfully turned what had been a matter of acute personal embarrassment to him—helping men like Szonyi back into Eastern Europe after the war—into their eventual downfall. They had been less than honest with Dulles. Their primary intention was not to continue fighting the Fascists but to establish their own positions, ready to take over once the war had been won. Now he was paying them back in the same coin, but one revalued a thousand times.

This is how Szonyi explained it to the people's court:

... During the war, political *émigrés* from almost every Central and Eastern European state, among them left-wing Communist groups, were staying in great numbers in Switzerland. Among the left-wing political *émigrés*, the intelligence organs of Great Britain, and especially of the United States of America, were doing very active work. . . . The American military strategic intelligence, the so-called Office of Strategic Services, had its European center in Switzerland. Its head was Allen Dulles, as representative in Europe. . . . In the summer of 1944 . . . it had become obvious that a part of the East European and Central European countries would be liberated by the Soviet troops. At that time, the American intelligence service ... began to concentrate on the task of bringing into its organization spies from the political *émigrés* there, especially from the left-wing Communist groups. The purpose of this was to infiltrate these people in the territories liberated by the Soviet troops, to carry out underground activity against the Communist parties there. It was in the course of this activity that I came into contact with the American spy organization. The chief helpmate and closest collaborator of Allen Dulles in his work of organizing spies from among the political

émigrés was Noel H. Field, who was officially the head of
an American relief organization in Switzerland ... called
the Unitarian Services Committee. ... His duty, as head
of the relief organization, was to extend financial help
and assistance to the political *émigrés* and through this
to establish connections and friendship with them and
do organization work for the American spy ring. ... My
group came to the conclusion that after the war we had
to take a position in Hungary within the Communist
party, and, in general, we would have to represent such a
political line as would make Hungary range herself on
the side of the United States. Lompar [a Yugoslav
diplomat] proposed to me in September 1944 that I
should enter into direct contact with OSS leader Allen
Dulles. Lompar and Field were active ... not only with
the Hungarian political *émigré* group but with other
political *émigré* groups, too. So I definitely knew that
they had established a similar contact with the Czechoslovak ... [and] Polish political *émigré* groups. ... My
formal enrollment into the American spy organization
took place at the end of November 1944, in Berne. At
this meeting, Dulles explained to me at length his political conception for the period after the war and told me
that the Communist parties would obviously become
government parties in a whole series of Eastern European countries which would be liberated by Soviet
troops. So support for an American orientation and the
American collaboration policy should be carried on first
of all within the Communist party. He asked me about
my chances of infiltrating into the Communist party in
Hungary. When I had given him adequate information
about that, he set me certain tasks. At this meeting at
the end of November 1944, despite there being no differences of opinion between us in the question of the
common activities, and though I entirely identified
myself with the point of view he explained to me, Dulles
showed me, as a means of terrorizing me, the receipt I
had signed on a previous occasion for Noel H. Field ...

for a subsidy I had received. I agreed with him that after
our return home we would remain in contact with each
other and I would use in this contact the cover name
"Peter" and he the cover name "Wagner."

Szonyi then went on to describe how he discovered
that Rajk was also an American agent, and how he made
contact with him and the plans they then made to destroy
the people's democracy established in Hungary.

Szonyi's statement provides a fascinating insight into
both Splinter Factor, as planned by the Americans, and
Soviet reaction to it, as well as indicating the subtlety with
which Russian show trials of this kind were organized. Virtually every statement made by Szonyi was true; it was
the gloss he was required to place upon his words, the
motives he adduced to himself and others, which turned
his narrative from being a factual statement of what had
actually occurred into a pack of lies.

Outside observers have always been intrigued by how
men like Rajk or Szonyi could go into court and, hour after
hour, talk of themselves in the most despicable terms, deni-
grate all their achievements, reveal themselves as traitors
to their country, knowing this act of abnegation was a foul
fraud upon themselves, their families and, in the final analysis, their country.

One of the Czech defendants of a later trial, ex-
deputy minister of trade Eugen Loebl, an urbane, highly
intelligent, sophisticated university lecturer, economist
and writer who went through this experience and somehow
emerged alive and sane at the end of a terrible ordeal,
could not really explain why he confessed to a long list of
imaginary crimes. He tried to describe the process:

... a Statement of Question and Answer was drawn up
giving all the questions the Judge and Prosecutor were

going to ask me and the answers I was to give. When I
learned them by heart, I was tested by one of the
officials, a miner from Ostran, called Drozd. He ... "produced" me, telling me if I was speaking loudly enough,
too slowly or too quickly. It appalls me now to think
that I was not even aware of the idiotic, degrading position I was in. ... All that man has inherited down the
ages, what he values most highly, what has become part
of his nature, what it is that actually makes him human
—all that had ceased to exist in me. ... I feel guilty that
I was not strong enough to stand up to the terror. I was
not justified in acting against my ideals, and I believe
that to the end of my life I shall not be able to forgive
myself that weakness. ... I was a completely normal
person, apart from the fact that I had ceased to be
human.*

Artur London, a fellow defendant of Loebl's who also
lived through and beyond this terrible experience to write
his story, has this to say:

Two or three days before the trial, I was taken into a
room where I found myself before a member of the
Party's Political Bureau, the Minister of Security, Karol
Bacilek. ... I heard him explain that the Party appealed
to me to stick to my statement as it was written in the
report for the court, that ... the national situation was
extremely serious, that there was a threat of war and
that the Party expected me to be guided by national and
Party interests; if I did so, my conduct would be taken
into account.

This confirmed my belief that if I denied anything
before the court, if I claimed to be innocent, nobody
would believe me and I would be hanged.

And then although you knew that you were an

* Eugen Loebl, *Sentenced and Tried* (London: Elek, 1969), pp.
19–20.

innocent and powerless victim in the hands of ruthless criminals ... you knew that beyond the courtroom, the interrogators, and the Soviet advisers, there was the Party with its mass of devoted members, the Soviet Union and its people who had performed so many sacrifices for the cause of Communism. There was the peace camp, the millions of combatants struggling for the same ideal the world over, the same socialist ideal to which you had devoted your whole life. You knew that the international situation was tense, that the cold war was raging, that everything could be used by the imperialists to spark off another war. As a conscientious Communist, you could not agree to become an "objective accomplice" of the imperialists.

Then you decided that, since all was lost, you might as well conceal your innocence and plead guilty.*

Later, describing the first day of the trial, London comments: "I . . . had no more human reactions than a piece of metal on a conveyor belt about to be crushed by a machine."

Like Loebl, he felt utterly dehumanized.

While there is no record of how they got their confessions, testimony of other Hungarian prisoners of that period indicates that their interrogations followed classic patterns. The method had been refined over the years inside the Soviet Union. First came the brutality, the humiliation of the subject—obviously always more effective the more important a man he was—the draining from him of any hope of relief. He would be asked to confess the most ludicrous crimes and would find that every detail of his life was being exhumed, every act twisted beyond recognition. Day after day he would rewrite his life story, and every slight difference from one version to another would

---

* Artur London, *On Trial* (London: Macdonald and Company, Ltd., 1970), pp. 257–258.

be exhaustively explored by his interrogators. Eventually driven by physical pain and mental suffering, he would start to lose track of the truth, his memory would falter; if he had been shown to be wrong on one minor point, perhaps he was wrong on others.

In the second stage the interrogator would change. The new man would be considerate and courteous. Perhaps the prisoner had not meant to work for the Americans, but had not his policies damaged the socialist cause, produced a rift inside the Soviet bloc, and had he not, therefore, perhaps innocently, assisted the imperialists? Was he not at least objectively guilty? Grateful for this new line of questioning, brought up to believe that the party was always right, prepared to accept that he made honest mistakes which, if the party said so, might have had catastrophic consequences, the prisoner would eagerly embrace his errors and freely confess to them and errors he didn't make.

Enter the third interrogator—as vicious as the first. What is this nonsense about objective guilt? How could the prisoner do such damage to the party and claim that he did not know what he was doing? Too late, the prisoner would realize the trap he had set himself and try to withdraw from the earlier confession, but he had already signed it and, moreover, signed it while he was being well treated. Completely lost, the prisoner would crumble and admit to anything just so he might be allowed to sit down or sleep uninterrupted for a few hours.

The fourth stage was designed merely to stiffen his resolve. The party had a specific duty for him. If he accepted the duty, it would show that he was not past redemption; if he did not, it would mark him as an incurable traitor. If he confessed freely, he would get a comparatively light sentence and, in due time, rejoin human society. If he did not, he would hang. The treatment of his family would also depend upon his cooperation: behave, and the party would look after them; make an exhibition in court, and they would suffer.

They used a subtly wicked technique on Rajk at the final stage of his interrogation. He was visited in his prison cell by his good friend Janos Kadar, the Hungarian minister of the interior, whose life had been saved by Rajk's wife during the war. Kadar promised Rajk that if he admitted his guilt in court, the death sentence passed on him would be purely fictitious and he would be able to live out the rest of his days in the Crimea. Rajk made the mistake of believing him.*

The public prosecutor, summing up, personified Rajk as "a common spy, an instrument of foreign powers, a conspirator, a bandit preparing for treachery." Describing his attempts to establish a treasonable conspiracy with the Yugoslavs, the prosecutor went on:

> ... it is in the light of these infamous plans, these infamous conditions, these conditions injuring our honor that we can best see the endeavor of the Western imperialist radios and press to make Rajk and his accomplices the representatives of some "national line." The representative of the national line, as far as the ruling circles of London and Washington and the spokesmen for the British and American imperialists are concerned, is a

---

* Kadar was subsequently arrested, imprisoned and tortured himself. After he was released and eventually became ruler of Hungary, he called on Rajk's widow and asked if she would forgive him. "I forgive," she said. "My husband would have been murdered in any case. But can you forgive yourself? If you want to live as a decent person, you must tell the world what you have told me." Janos Kadar never has.

man who has for eighteen years been a professional informer and traitor who sold his fatherland retail and wholesale to foreign imperialists and chiefs of espionage, from Noel H. Field to Allen Dulles, through the Deuxième Bureau and the Gestapo to the intelligence organizations of Tito and Rankovitch.

Honored People's Court, a logical consequence of the fact that Rajk and his accomplices conspired to betray Hungary's independence is that they wanted to tear our country out of the powerful democratic peace camp and to turn her against the Soviet Union.

Operation Splinter Factor was to get another direct acknowledgment in the prosecutor's final address. Addressing himself to denials made by American diplomats who were alleged during the trial to be CIA agents who had contacted either Rajk or his fellow defendants, the prosecutor declared:

What basis do they have for denying that Mr. Allen Dulles had something to do with Tibor Szonyi's espionage groups when Dulles's brother, John Foster Dulles, announced the so-called Operation X project for organizing underground movements—in the people's democracies in the spring of 1948, that is, at the very time that Tito and Rajk and company intensified their activities?

The substance of this secret plan was summarized by the Swiss paper *Die Tat* in its issue of April 26th, 1949, after John Foster Dulles, as follows: "The West attempted first of all to penetrate into the cadres and elite of the ruling classes of the people's democracies and it is said they succeeded in this beyond their hopes. . . ."

Well, the material of the whole trial is contained in this confession of a few lines. . . . Here the practical execution of the project the American imperialists called Operation X was unveiled.

The prosecutor concluded:

> Our people demand death for the traitors, and I, as the
> representative of the prosecuting authority, identify
> myself with this demand. ... A verdict is called for from
> which every imperialist spy and traitor will learn what
> he must expect if he dares to raise his hand against our
> people's republic. ...

In his final plea, Laszlo Rajk had this to say for himself before sentence was passed:

> In the first place, before the people's court passes its ver-
> dict, to avoid and eliminate any misunderstanding, I
> must point out that everything I ever did and commit-
> ted, I committed always on my own decision, after free
> deliberation. ... In conclusion, I fully agree with most of
> the statements of the prosecutor; of course, I am not
> here thinking of the secondary and in any case unimpor-
> tant details, but of the substance. Now, precisely
> because of this, I declare in advance that whatever the
> sentence of the people's court may be in my case, I shall
> consider this sentence just.

That sentence was read out by the judge, Dr. Janko,
at 9:45 on the morning of September 24, eight days after
the start of the trial. Laszlo Rajk was condemned to death
by hanging and was executed on October 14 along with
Tibor Szonyi and Andras Szalai on gallows specially built
in the prison yard in Central Budapest.

So Laszlo Rajk was finally crushed by the system for
which he had sacrificed everything. Not till 1945, when he
was thirty-six years old, was it safe for Rajk to be what he
was, a Communist. His triumph was short-lived, for four
years later he was dead.

For a short time, the Communist rank and file, even the intellectuals, believed in his guilt. But gradually the rumors of how confessions were extracted from political prisoners who were now being arrested by the hundreds began to filter down. Events in neighboring Bulgaria ignited the spark of doubt, and the gradual realization that the Communist party was now feeding on its young began to bear down upon a horrified population. This was not how they imagined it would be.

Chapter 10
The Men Who Fought Back

As heroes they made an unlikely pair, yet heroes of this story they undoubtedly are. The first, Traicho Kostov of Bulgaria, deputy premier, economic czar of his country and the natural successor to the aging and ailing President Georgi Dimitroff; the second, Wladyslaw Gomulka, who, until 1947, had been general secretary of the Polish Communist party and the only possible rival to President Bierut.

Unlike the gay, witty Laszlo Rajk, with his passion for football and good clothes, Kostov and Gomulka had no time for frivolities. It is true that Gomulka was rumored to have had an affair with his secretary and that Kostov, too, had an eye for a pretty girl, but such lapses in these otherwise sternly puritanical men were hardly remarkable on the continent of Europe.

145

Otherwise, Kostov and Gomulka were men of granite, certain that they alone were right. Bad mixers and uneasy in the company of ordinary people, they were not particularly appealing men. Yet both, in their separate ways, against all their own inclinations, became great popular heroes throughout Eastern Europe—one because of the manner of his death, and the other because of the way he lived.

Each in his own way proved himself to be bigger and perhaps even more durable than Joseph Stalin. Kostov and Gomulka defeated Stalin as well as Allen Dulles. Dulles wished to leave Eastern Europe devoid of hope so that he could introduce a pro-American, anti-Soviet form of government. Traicho Kostov and Wladyslaw Gomulka destroyed that possibility by giving people enough hope so they could endure. Dulles proved that it was possible to manipulate great nations and even whole blocs. What he did not, and indeed could not, make allowances for was the stubbornness of two dyed-in-the-wool apparatchiks, lacking in imagination and vision, mistrustful of people's ability to control their own destiny, and yet so courageous that to this day they stand supreme as a monument to the triumph of the individual over an all-consuming power.

What makes Kostov and Gomulka so interesting in the context of this story is that they had fallen from power months before Operation Splinter Factor had distorted Stalin's view of his East European possessions.

Wladyslaw Gomulka was the first to go. He had become first secretary of the Polish Communist party during the war, almost by accident. Twice Moscow had sent in its own man for the job, the importance of which was undoubted in a country on Russia's borders. For Stalin knew, from the very earliest days of the war when the Curzon Line argument first came up, that the great

divide would become a battlefield between Poles of East
and West orientation. Each of Moscow's nominees for the
job was killed and, while communications were down
between Poland and Moscow for a period of six months,
Gomulka was installed in power. He was not the man
Stalin would have chosen.

Immediately, Gomulka saw that the Polish Communist party (officially it was the Polish Workers' party, the
PPR) had been in the past more concerned with playing
off old scores against the Home Army, backed by the
London government, than with fighting the Nazis. Indeed,
there were some ugly examples of collaboration between
the Communists and the Fascist invader which are a per-
petual stain on the honor of the Polish Communist party.
Gomulka put a stop to that immediately, even though the
orders for some of these more discreditable episodes had
come from Moscow itself.

Meanwhile, Stalin was preparing the Lublin Committee as the provisional government of Poland, made up
entirely of men who had served the war in Moscow and
including men like their leader, Boleslaw Bierut, who had
been in the pay of the Russian security police for many
years. With little support from the Poles themselves, the
committee looked to Moscow, who had put them into
power, for protection and counsel, and viewed with fear
and suspicion any Pole without its particular background.
The committee was right to do so, for the feeling was
mutual.

Nevertheless, the Moscow Poles needed a Gomulka to
provide their government with a vestige of respectability.
His patriotism could not be denied; he had lived in Poland
throughout the war and had a fine reputation as a resistance fighter and as a man who stood up for Poland against
the Russians. When Soviet officers who parachuted into

Poland to help the resistance refused to accept Polish orders, Gomulka wrote personally to Stalin, complaining of their conduct. When, for a period of the war, Stalin was negotiating with London Poles and cut off arms supplies to Polish Communists, Gomulka did not bother to conceal, again in letters direct to Stalin, his contempt for a policy which was sacrificing people for politics.

After the war Gomulka, however unpopular he may have been in Moscow, was important to the Communists, dealing as they were with a population that regarded them with loathing. He had the prestige to create a different atmosphere. But from the outset, it was an uneasy partnership. When Russian soldiers were caught looting, Gomulka ordered them shot on sight. When the Russians began dismantling German machinery and industrial plants in the new areas which Poland received from Germany in place of the land she gave away to the Russians in the East, and shipping these to Russia, Gomulka ordered a halt and forced the Russians to negotiate. The result was hardly a Polish triumph, but at least he stopped the wholesale stripping of new Polish assets with no compensation.

On the international front, Gomulka, like Marshal Tito, was opposed to the creation of the Cominform and saw the danger inherent in an organization which would rigidly tie all of its members to Moscow; he expressed his opposition in 1947 during the early months of debate on this topic more strongly and clearly than did Tito himself. When Tito was expelled from the Cominform in June 1948 at the famous meeting in Bucharest, Gomulka expressed his disapproval by staying away. That was too much for Moscow, who insisted that he be removed from his post; at a meeting of the Polish Central Committee in the same month, he was harshly criticized for "nationalist tendencies" and persuaded to take indefinite leave on the grounds of poor health.

Two weeks later, to the horror of his colleagues, Gomulka informed them he was well again and calmly resumed his task as general secretary. It was a splendid gesture of defiance, but he was not to get away with it. This time he was removed from office by a vote of the full Central Committee and forced into retirement. His friends and supporters went with him as the career of this tough and self-righteous Pole seemed to come to an end.

Traicho Kostov's story had a similar ring to it. On June 17, 1947, the Central Committee of the Bulgarian Communist party celebrated his fiftieth birthday with a paean of praise which would have made Nero blush:

> Great are your achievements, Comrade Traicho Kostov ... your deep Marxist-Leninist theoretical knowledge, your great culture, your famous industry and steadfastness, your modesty, your iron will, your unquestionable loyalty toward the party and the working class. ... You are today one of the most loved and respected leaders of our party, a great statesman and builder of new Bulgaria. ...

On March 27, 1949, less than two years later, the same Central Committee announced that Kostov had been dismissed as deputy premier and chairman of the National Economic and Finance Committee because he had pursued an "insincere and unfriendly policy toward the USSR" in trade negotiations. He was appointed director of the National Library, and it was hoped he would sink into decent obscurity.

Kostov, like Gomulka, was a nationalist through and through. When he negotiated trade agreements with the Russians, he did so as a Bulgarian, seeking to get the best conditions for Bulgaria and the best prices for Bulgarian products. In the eyes of the Russians, his greatest crime was that he refused to divulge the cost price of Bulgarian goods, which the Russians said they needed in order to fix a fair price. Kostov claimed they needed these figures in order to offer the lowest possible price—and that he was not prepared to accept.

He was in trouble, just like Gomulka, for his international policies, too. For a long time he had advocated a federation of the Balkans, which Russia bitterly resisted. Stalin could see a federation of this kind becoming rich and powerful enough to be able to cast itself adrift and pursue an independent line from Moscow.

The fascinating aspect of the Gomulka and Kostov cases is that when these men fell out of favor with Moscow, in mid-1948 to about the spring of 1949, no one suggested that they were spies or saboteurs who should be put on trial for their lives. All Moscow required was that they should abandon the portfolios which had put them into opposition with the Central Committee and retire from all active politics.

Operation Splinter Factor was to change all of that. From the moment Noel Field was marked down as an American agent whose object was to drive the satellites out of the Soviet orbit, the actions of all of those who had disagreed with the Moscow line in the past became not merely mistaken but considerably more sinister. These men were either active American agents, part of the Field conspiracy, or they were acting, whether or not they knew it, for American interests.

Furthermore, it was not easy to tell which they were, since the agents were advocating the very policies which the so-called nationalists had been advocating since 1945. So blurred had the dividing line become between deliberate acts of treason and treasonable acts occasioned by what the Russians would regard as political immaturity that it became not only impossible to distinguish the two but positively in the Russian interest not to do so. For, once Stalin accepted that the policies for the satellites being advocated by American agent Noel Field were the same as those advocated by the nationalists, then the treason and the heresy became one and the same and had to be punished with equal ferocity.

So it was no accident that Wladyslaw Gomulka, who had been sacked in June 1948, only came under investigation in June 1949, a day after Noel Field's arrest. Nor was it an accident that Traicho Kostov, made a director of the National Library in March 1949 and permitted to accept honorable retirement, was, a month after Field's arrest, expelled from the party and, two months later, arrested for "grave crimes against the state." Operation Splinter Factor was not going to permit either of these two men to disappear into decent obscurity.

The Kostov case was immediately and directly linked with Noel Field, who, though he did not know Kostov, did know a great many of the people around Kostov and provided their names during his interrogation by the Hungarians. Kostov, it was alleged, had held Trotskyite views since 1933, had "given away his comrades" when arrested by the pro-German Bulgarian police in 1942, and, by the end of 1944, had made contact with the British intelligence service, "under whose instructions and advice he subsequently carried on his hostile activity against the Republic." After the war, he had established contact with Yugoslav leaders, had tried to disrupt economic and trade relations between Bulgaria and the USSR, and had sought to overthrow the established government in Bulgaria with the assistance of the Yugoslavs. Now he was to be put on trial as a British agent, and also on the stand with him were most economists of any renown.

When, on December 7, the trial in Sofia opened, every-

one knew what to expect. Kostov and his fellow defendants
would plead guilty, openly confessing to every word on the
indictment and much else besides. But Traicho did not
oblige. He dared plead not guilty and go back in open court
upon the "confession" he had made under duress in prison
or, as the London Communist daily, *The Daily Worker*,
preferred to put it:

> With supreme cynicism he contradicted even his own
> oral testimony to the contrary at the trial by declaring:
> "I have always cherished admiration for the Soviet
> Union." ... With complete disregard of the detailed guilt
> acknowledged in his own written confession, Kostov
> remained faithful to the last to his Anglo-American mas-
> ters.

The Daily Worker did not reveal that the court immediately rose in consternation after his not-guilty plea; that
when it resumed, Kostov's defense counsel apologized for
his client's behavior; and that the Bulgarian press, who
were giving the trial maximum coverage, somehow managed to overlook the fact that the chief defendant had
actually denied the charges.

Kostov was not invited to take further part in the
deliberations concerning him. The court relied upon his
written confession for the evidence they required. After
a trial which lasted a week, the judge asked Kostov if he
had anything to say before passing sentence. Kostov did:
"I regard it as my duty, prompted by my conscience, to say
in this court and before the Bulgarian people that I was
never in the services of the British espionage, that I never
took part in the plans of any plotters, that I have always
given honor and respect to Russia. ..."

"Stop it!" shouted the presiding judge, and proceeded
to sentence him to death. Despite the Bulgarian press, it
didn't take long for news of Kostov's defiance to sweep

through Bulgaria and into the other countries of Eastern Europe. The authorities desperately tried to stem these damaging rumors by publishing a so-called death-bed confession in which Kostov not only apologized "for the wrongness of my conduct before the Supreme Court," but also confessed a second time to the charges. As Kostov was dead—hanged in the prison yard in Sofia on December 17, 1949—he was unable to refute his confession this time, but his staunch courage in court ensured that the people would do it for him.

Communists had, by and large, tended to believe the Rajk trial. It had been carefully prepared, evidence was presented which helped make the charges stick, and the confessions themselves, though perhaps overdrawn, were not intrinsically improbable, at least to the believers. But when those same Communists heard that Kostov had pleaded not guilty and that the court had refused to listen, preferring a written confession from a prison cell, then the rumors that confessions were being beaten out of the defendants could no longer be ignored. They reviewed in their minds the Rajk trial and all the other political trials, and they were never to believe again.

For what Kostov had done was to show that it was possible for the individual to stand up in the face of even as mighty a nation as the Soviet Union. He didn't win—no one who goes to his death upon the gallows can claim to have won anything—but the cause to which he had devoted his life did emerge the victor. He strengthened the resolve of other opposition Communists like himself; for many years more they had to remain underground, but all the time they were buoyed up by the knowledge that in the end it is the individual who counts.

Wladyslaw Gomulka was quick to benefit from the Kostov debacle. It was apparent that the Bulgarians had botched the whole process; Stalin was furious, and the Soviet advisers who had handled the trial were sent into exile in Siberia for their incompetence. The lesson was quickly learned. In the future not only would defendants have to be adequately prepared but the evidence submitted against them would have to bear some semblance to reason.

The Poles were determined not to make that kind of mistake with Gomulka, who was also now heavily implicated as a Fieldist. Again, he never met either of them, but the Fields did know several Gomulka supporters. This was, of course, Jozef Swiatlo's home territory, and he could be expected to make the most of it. Unfortunately, however, Hermann Field was not proving a cooperative witness. Though the Poles were convinced that Lord Layton's British Trust, which had employed Hermann in Katowice in the late thirties, was a cover for British intelligence (a belief still obstinately held to this day by many members of the Communist party), it was impossible to implicate Hermann Field in any serious way, as the Hungarians were able to do with his brother, Noel.

The Poles whom Noel Field named had been rounded up months ago, and though several committed suicide or ended up in lunatic asylums, their minds having been broken by the ferocity of their tortures, most refused to implicate Gomulka in any way.

Nevertheless, Gomulka had to be arrested—Stalin demanded it. Totally convinced that any nationalist was also an American agent, he told his security men: "If they are too clever to leave any evidence around for you to find, you must be clever enough to find evidence which they did not know existed." It was a straight invitation to manufacture the proof.

As elsewhere, the number-one target was implicated

by a subordinate. In Poland the man chosen for the
Gomulka case was General Marian Spychalski. Because he
was Gomulka's closest colleague and friend on the Politburo, tremendous pressure was exerted upon him to dis-
avow Gomulka. This he did at the Politburo meeting in
1948 at which Gomulka was expelled. When Spychalski
had betrayed him, Gomulka knew he was alone.

By 1951 the decision had been made that Gomulka
had to be arrested. But in order to do that, Spychalski had
to be broken. Spychalski, who had been sacked as minister
of defense long ago and who was then working as a civil
engineer in Wroclaw, was picked up by Colonel Swiatlo.
Recalling Spychalski's arrest, Swiatlo later said:

> So when Spychalski, after arriving in Wroclaw, entered
> his house, he already found me in his room. He was fol-
> lowed by his bodyguard, who could see me and who
> knew what it was all about, for they were working with
> me. Spychalski stood facing me with his bodyguard
> behind him. We knew each other personally. He greeted
> me, shook my hand, and I held onto his hand, and did
> not let go. My agents searched him. Spychalski went a
> little pale and I told him: "We shall go to Warsaw, com-
> rade." He did not resist, and I took him by car ... to the
> prison in our villa in Miedzeszyn.

Once in prison, Spychalski proved to be of sterner
stuff than he had previously indicated and refused in any
way to compromise Gomulka.

Fortunately, Gomulka was able to call upon his two
great strengths. First, there was nothing in his past to
show that he had behaved in any way other than that of a
loyal Pole and a loyal Communist. He was without a single
skeleton in his cupboard. Second, he was able to inspire
loyalty in those around him. All of his closest friends, when

arrested in order to incriminate him, refused to say anything at all to his discredit. He was finally picked up
because the Russians insisted, not because there was any
evidence against him.

Colonel Swiatlo, who was called in to make the arrest,
eventually related the story of Gomulka's arrest and subsequent imprisonment:

> For proof of Gomulka's guilt, we also got in touch with
> the fraternal parties. I talked with the chiefs of Hungar-
> ian and Czech security and I examined people arrested
> in connection with those trials. . . . I investigated the
> imprisoned Field family and nowhere could I obtain any
> proof of Gomulka's guilt.
>
> In July 1951, it was decided to arrest Gomulka.
>
> Radkiewicz called me into his office [and] . . . gave
> me orders to go to Krynica, arrest Gomulka, and bring
> him back to Warsaw. He said that this was on Bierut's
> order. I was to induce Gomulka to go to Warsaw with
> me of his own accord. . . .
>
> It was 7 A.M. when I arrived in Krynica and entered
> Gomulka's room in the New Resort Hotel. His wife,
> Zofia . . . had gone into town for a short while. Gomulka
> knew me very well. Therefore, I entered, said "Good
> morning," and added that I had come on orders from the
> party to take him with me to Warsaw. At first, Gomulka
> refused, saying that he was now on vacation and that he
> did not want to go to Warsaw. In the meantime, his wife
> returned and made some fuss. . . . Thus, I talked with
> Comrade Wladyslaw and with his wife from 7 till 10
> A.M., trying to persuade them that they should go . . .
> with me voluntarily. Eventually, Gomulka got dressed,
> the three of us got into the car, and we started out.
>
> I planned the trip so that we would not enter
> Warsaw in broad daylight. It was neither agreeable nor
> convenient for me to have all Warsaw see me in the com-
> pany of the former secretary-general in such circum-

stances. Therefore, I often stopped along the way. In the meantime, confusion reigned in Warsaw. Almost every half hour, Bierut and Minc telephoned Romkowski inquiring about what was going on. They could not account for those few hours which I spent stopping on the road. Anxious and frightened, they ordered that the radio car should be sent to meet me and establish contact with me. I passed that radio car between Kielce and Radom, but I did not stop. What was the use?

I arrived in town during the night and took Gomulka and his wife directly to their places of detention. Gomulka was placed in Miedzeszyn, near Warsaw, in a special villa under the control of the Tenth Department of the Security Ministry. . . . I placed Gomulka's wife, Zofia . . . in a neighboring house. I was personally responsible . . . for the security and well-being of Gomulka and his wife.

. . . He lived in a room with barred windows and got good food, books and the periodical *Problems* [*Problemy*]. He was not permitted to receive newspapers. In the wall of the room was a Judas window through which a guard watched him all the time. . . . Gomulka's health did not deteriorate badly, though he had stomach troubles, and the leg which had been shot by the police before the war was getting stiff.

Gomulka's arrest and detention at Miedzeszyn began a series of complications and confusions in the Politburo. First of all, no one of the party leadership had the courage to talk with him. They were simply afraid of him. . . . As a result, Gomulka remained at Miedzeszyn for almost three months in almost complete isolation, and absolutely no one interrogated him.

Finally, a decision was taken in the Politburo. Security Vice-Minister Romkowski and the chief of the Tenth Department, Colonel Fejgin, were assigned to talk to Gomulka. . . . Up to my departure in December, 1953—that is, for two and a half years—Gomulka's examination did not fill more than fifteen full working days. Through that time, no one from the party talked to him.

During the interrogations, Gomulka did not admit anything more than what he had stated at the Plenum. ... He accused Bierut and his clique of everything and attacked them and the party for collaboration with the Nazis during the occupation and for their internal struggles. He accused them of having sold out almost all the Communists arrested in Russia. I know he was very much concerned with their fate.

So Gomulka went one stage further than Kostov. Kostov had confessed in prison and withdrawn that confession in open court. Gomulka refused to confess in prison. Although he was never tortured or maltreated, it is unlikely he would have confessed to false accusations even under extreme pressure. He was so relentlessly honest and so totally convinced of his strength that Warsaw's political jokesters let it be known that the new atomic icebreaker being developed by the Russians would be tested first on Comrade Wladyslaw. He wore out teams of interrogators, never slipping for a moment, never dropping his guard.

Suddenly and unexpectedly, Poland's tough, withdrawn, unapproachable Wladyslaw Gomulka became personified in people's minds with the struggle for Polish independence. If he crumbled, then so would the nation. But he didn't, and Poland still had a future. Splinter Factor had met its match at last.

Chapter 11

Korea: The Bitter Harvest

By the time Wladyslaw Gomulka had been arrested by
Colonel Swiatlo, Operation Splinter Factor was already
getting out of hand. Where once Dulles had been able to
manipulate events with the perfect control of a puppeteer,
now, in 1950, the whole operation was rushing downhill
under its own crazed momentum. Dulles himself, in fact,
was momentarily out of the picture altogether. The CIA
had grown so much in size and importance that an outsider
like Dulles could no longer exercise day-to-day authority
over anything. Those in the agency who knew about Operation Splinter Factor were satisfied that it was working as
well as—and indeed better than—anyone had hoped. The
Fields were forgotten. No one knew whether they were
alive or dead, and no one much cared. All that mattered
was that the hypothesis which had launched the operation

had proved to be triumphantly correct. Life inside the
Communist bloc was becoming increasingly difficult; the
Stalinists were in the ascendancy everywhere, and the
people were known to be chafing under intolerable political
and economic restrictions. Reports of industrial unrest
inside Eastern Europe percolated through to Washington
almost weekly. The counterrevolution really did seem to be
at hand.

If Dulles himself had been at the helm during this cru-
cial period, he almost certainly would have detected the
agency's critical error of judgment. Being such a complete
professional in the business, he would have recognized the
risks inherent in any intelligence operation in which control and direction are lost. It was time to reassess Splinter
Factor, to decide whether the events stemming from the
arrest of the Fields were not snowballing to dangerous proportions. But this was never done; instead, the news of
each new arrest was greeted in Washington with a silent
cheer and chalked up as another triumph on the Splinter
Factor scoreboard. Yet Splinter Factor had been left far
behind. The new victims were unknown to the CIA;
whether their arrests helped or hindered the Western
cause became a matter of indifference.

Yet from the very outset Dulles had recognized the
prime necessity: always to keep sight of the ultimate goal.
(This was his trademark throughout his entire professional
life, and it alone set him apart from his contemporaries as a
man of genius.) He also saw the inherent dangers of med-
dling with such an explosive character as Joseph Stalin.

The fact is that the success of Operation Splinter
Factor had seriously disturbed the old man in the Kremlin.
Spies, saboteurs and traitors stood all around him. He
could trust nothing and no one. The enemy was at the
gates, and war seemed to him to be inevitable. In September 1949 the entire world knew that Stalin possessed the

atomic bomb; by November it knew why he believed it necessary. At a Cominform meeting in Warsaw, American imperialism was seen as an "international conspiracy" as evidenced by the Rajk and Kostov trials. That plot had to be squashed. Seeing in the Fieldist conspiracy merely the first drive by the Americans to separate Russia from her new European possessions, Stalin began to believe that the American military assault would not be long in coming. The only way to save the satellites would be to drive the Americans from European soil. President Roosevelt had assured him at Yalta that the Americans would stay on the continent of Europe for only eighteen months after the end of World War II. But they were still there, in increasing numbers, and talking of rearming West Germany as well as setting up military alliances with Russia's erstwhile wartime allies. Stalin regarded the Truman Doctrine as an unacceptable breach of faith, the Marshall Plan as an attempt at the economic enslavement of the European states, and the formation of NATO as a piece of naked aggression. And as if that were not enough, the Americans had cleverly planted their agents—men like Rajk—into the highest positions of authority inside Stalin's own apparatus.

It doesn't matter if one regards all of that as the ravings of a man in the advanced stages of schizophrenic paranoia, or the partly genuine grievances of a leader whose hopes and ambitions were misunderstood by his ex-wartime allies. Neither should it have mattered then. It was sufficient that he was the czar of Russia and her dominions, and that whether or not he was a tyrant, he and his complex personality should have been taken into consideration. It was not, and Operation Splinter Factor was to tip him over the edge.

As more reports came in of traitors arrested by his secret police, Stalin began to plan his counterattack. The

Americans had to be driven off the continent of Europe, and if that meant World War III, then so be it.

Now Stalin went on the offensive. In Europe, the Warsaw Pact forces were preparing for the military occupation of West Germany, with a roll-on contingent to take on Belgium, France and Britain if any of these powers interfered. Stalin's most experienced generals and diplomats told him that if he applied enough pressure, the Americans would leave quietly. No American government would go to war in order to defend European cities (though they might in order to attack Russia). A proclamation to the Americans was already prepared. While it spoke of Russian friendship toward the American people it stated that this friendship was jeopardized by the fact that the Americans were massing more and more armaments on Russia's borders daily. Russia had made sacrifices during the war and she was determined not to have made them in vain. The Russian people had the right to expect the Germans to be neutralized; if this was done, the peace of the world would be assured.

The Americans would be given twenty-four hours to signify that they would not stand in the way of the Red Army as it moved into position into West Germany. They would be given seven days to move out of Europe altogether. The spine-chilling prospects of nuclear war did not seem to bother Stalin unduly. He was sure that Russia could survive it and that America could not. The American character, he believed, could not withstand a direct hit on New York City.*

The first rounds of the war-that-never-was were fired

* I recognize that this is a controversial statement and will not be accepted by many historians, but after a lengthy series of interviews with prominent men inside the Warsaw Pact general staff during the period, I have no doubt that such a plan existed and that it was taken most seriously by Stalin. It was not merely a contingency plan. Stalin's death prevented it from being put into practice.

on June 25, 1950, as North Korean troops crossed over into South Korea and precipitated what is now known as the Korean War.

To Americans, the Korean War has always been regarded as a purely local attempt by international communism to increase its sphere of influence. But to the Russians it was something else altogether. It was a deliberately stage-managed coup, both as a test of America's will to resist and as a method of distracting attention from Stalin's more important designs in Europe.

It was a brilliant stroke, militarily and diplomatically. It is only just now beginning to dawn upon historians of this era that the fact that the Russian delegate was not in his seat during the U.N. debates that permitted a United Nations force under American command to fight the North Koreans was not a dreadful mistake by Russia's foreign-policy makers. Quite the contrary, if Russia had attended any of the debates (which she easily could have done) she would have been forced to exercise her veto.* The result would almost certainly have been that the Americans would have had to fight it alone, not under the blue flag of the United Nations. If America had done that, as a matter of prestige Russia would have had to go in on the side of the Koreans, but Russia was not yet ready to face the implications of that. Indeed, the Russian strategy was to gain as much as possible without inviting a direct confrontation with the U.S. Army.

As it was, the Soviets, by cynically using the North

* If the Soviet delegate, Jacob Malik, had been present when the Security Council debated the first resolution condemning the aggression, then the Soviet veto could have been used to defeat it. Of course, he could not have been there on time, since the emergency debate was called within twenty-four hours of the attack. Furthermore, Russia had withdrawn her delegate from the Security Council just over five months previously because the China seat was held by Formosa. But he certainly could have arrived in time for the second vote, which legalized a U.N. military response, three days later, and there is no question

Koreans, were able to inveigle America into a war in a dis-
tant country which she knew little about. Russia, behind
the shadow cast by the war, was able to mass her troops,
organize full-scale Warsaw Pact exercises, produce new
weapons and give them to the Koreans to test in the field
—all under the guise not of an attack upon West Germany
but of a reaction to the increased international tension.

Though it may seem an oversimplification to say that
Operation Splinter Factor indirectly caused the Korean
War, it is not an unjustifiable statement. It was Operation
Splinter Factor which produced the spark: it fed Stalin's
paranoia. He needed this war because, after the terrible
political reverses of the show trials, he had to have a victory for international communism. He had to show not
merely the West but back sliders in his own camp that he,
not the Americans, represented the future.

Though it was played out in Asia, the Korean War
was in reality a European conflict; Korean and Chinese
soldiers fought and were killed on behalf of European
interests. Of course, U.N. troops died as well, but their
deaths were almost accidental. Relations between East and
West had become so tense that there *had* to be a war to
relieve the unbearable strain. Korea was a convenient area
to stage it. It had the advantage of being far enough away
from Europe and America to ensure that white civilians
didn't actually get killed, and remote enough so that no

---

that he could have arrived in time for the third, several days later still,
setting up a U.N. joint command.

The question which needs to be asked is: Did the Russians, in
fact, make a mistake at all? Did they overlook such basic provisions
of the U.N. Charter which they themselves had drawn up? Did they
forget the negative power of the veto which they had used so consistently and so effectively ever since the U.N. was brought into being?
The Russians had plenty of time to think—unlike the Americans, who,
faced with a sudden, unexpected attack, reacted with remarkable speed
and efficiency. Sophisticated Washington opinion now takes the view
that the Russians were playing a very clever game; they baited a trap
and saw the Americans truly hooked.

reverse, on either side, would merit the use of atomic
bombs in the Western hemisphere to uphold national
honor. While both sides fired up the ambitions of their
respective allies in Korea, the Russians persuaded the
North to steal the march.

Stalin was not one to think well of his fellow men. If
comrades like Rajk were traitors to the cause, they were
motivated not by doctrine but by opportunism. Stalin felt
he had to show who the master was, and he chose a small,
underdeveloped country in Asia in which to flex his mus-
cles.

If Splinter Factor influenced the outbreak of the war,
then the war also had a decisive influence upon the operation itself. The North Korean attack on June 25, 1950,
caught the U.S. administration completely by surprise.
Though the CIA had been reporting the buildup of North
Korean troops for some time, it had failed to predict that
an invasion across the 38th Parallel was imminent. In a
major sense, the criticism immediately leveled against the
CIA was unfair, as the agency was operating in an area
where General Douglas MacArthur "executed" messengers
who brought bad news.

And while MacArthur was in the ascendancy it was
unthinkable that he should be the scapegoat. So the agency's able and honest chief, Admiral Hillenkoeter, was
shunted into retirement and General Bedell "Beetle"
Smith was called in to pick up the pieces. Smith's first
administrative act on taking over in October 1950 was to
take the 1949 Dulles-Jackson-Correa report from the files,
where it had been ever since President Truman had
pigeonholed it. Next, he asked its two principal authors,
Dulles and Jackson, to come to Washington and imple-
ment their own recommendations.

It was one of the most important moments in Dulles's

life, for at last, in becoming number-three man at the CIA, he was in sight of his inheritance. Smith wisely left the job of intelligence to Jackson and Dulles while he concentrated upon the much-needed internal reform and, most important of all, established new lines of communication between the White House and the Pentagon so that when the CIA spoke, it was listened to. Dulles and Jackson, who both had the highest respect for him, let him get on with this essential task while they got down to the real business at hand.

Dulles saw quickly that the agency professionals had been seriously concerned by warlike preparations but that up till then neither the president nor Congress had cared to listen to their warnings. NATO and its European staff officers simply didn't believe that the agency was capable of producing any worthwhile intelligence at all. Certainly any tale of Communist aggression smacked too much of a typical American "Red under the bed" scare to be taken seriously. The Americans led by Joint Chief of Staff General Omar Bradley regarded the CIA report—that the Russians believed the Americans would not fight for the integrity of Europe—not as a piece of intelligence to be evaluated but as a direct assault on the honor of the American people.

The new management at the CIA saw immediately that while Korea was grabbing the headlines, the real problem still lay in Europe. Korea, they realized, was a cover for Stalin's eventual designs on Europe. Dulles himself called for the Splinter Factor files the moment his foot was inside the front door of the agency. The urgency of the international situation required an urgent solution, and Splinter Factor—which, since the death of Kostov at the end of 1949, had sunk into the background—was one available weapon which the CIA could profitably employ.

Unaware that the operation was in danger of rebounding, unperturbed that so far there had been little sign of the popular revolt inside Eastern Europe which he had predicted, Dulles saw with some clarity that if Stalin could be persuaded to see the unreliability of his allies, he might be forced to postpone his invasion plans.

Already morale throughout Eastern Europe was at rock bottom. Production was falling; people went about their daily tasks in a mood of sullen resentment. No government was liked; no party official or minister could count upon popular support. Stalin's problems in maintaining a united front against the "imperialists" were mounting daily, and Dulles saw it as his duty to increase his difficulties. Furthermore, Dulles did not doubt that the explosion would come one day. Already CIA-sponsored Washington lobbyists were preparing the ground for what was subsequently known as the Kersten Amendment, an amendment to the 1952 armed forces bill. Special units to be trained and barracked in Germany, all of East European origin, were to come to the aid of insurrectionary movements behind the Iron Curtain, provide professional support for the rebels and help reestablish democracy after the counterrevolution, which Dulles was sure would not be long in coming.

These were heady days. Even though nuclear war was still a distinct possibility, even though it looked as if the Russians might move into Western Europe, Americans like Dulles seemed to come alive with a new sense of confidence. Communism, as far as they could see, had been rejected wherever people still had a free choice. Where it existed, it did so only with the help of the secret police. It had failed to capture the minds and the hearts of great populations. The tyranny had been exposed.

But there was more work to be done. Russia was still

capable of waging world war; Stalin was still capable of unleashing a nuclear holocaust upon Western Europe. The fight had to be taken to the enemy with a new sense of fervor. So this time when Operation Splinter Factor was to be revived it would be more sophisticated: the targets would be selected with greater care, the purpose more clearly defined.

In all of Eastern Europe only Czechoslovakia had managed to escape the full wrath of Stalin. Revolt was already simmering; accustomed to a Western-style democracy, the Czech population chafed uncomfortably under the stern rules of its Communist masters. Turn Stalin's eyes to Czechoslovakia, and he would have no time or inclination for adventures elsewhere. Bring the Czech population out into the streets against their Communist rulers, and the rest of Eastern Europe would follow.

Newly installed in his office in Washington, Allen Dulles called his men together and planned Operation Splinter Factor—Target Czechoslovakia. It was the start of a bloodbath.

Chapter 12
Target Czechoslovakia

Klement Gottwald was not an old man, though he gave every such appearance. He no longer drank spirits merely to ease the burden of high office. There was a despairing quality about his drinking now, as if survival itself were dependent upon it. His once considerable political skill had been coarsened by the personality cult he had erected around himself as a protection from his own weaknesses. He had acquiesced in so many little crimes—because at the time he had allowed himself to be persuaded that the future of Czechoslovakia depended upon it—that he could no longer distinguish between justice and injustice. The president of Czechoslovakia was, in short, an empty shell. All the compassion, understanding and love had long since been drained from him and replaced by a morbid preoccupation with his own fate.

Klement Gottwald had once been a remarkable man. Born of a peasant family in Moravia, he was sent to Vienna at the age of twelve to relatives as an apprentice carpenter. During the First World War, he was conscripted into the Austro-Hungarian army, rose to the rank of sergeant and fought against the Russians on the Carpathian front. But he deserted and joined the newly formed Czech army and after demobilization worked in a factory and became shop steward and secretary of the local branch of the Social Democratic party. The party split, and out of the schism emerged the Czech Communist party, of which Gottwald became a founding member. In 1929, at the age of thirty-three, he became its secretary-general, a post he held until his death, and also an M.P. in the Czech parliament.

The Czechoslovakia in which he had his political apprenticeship and the Czechoslovakia he came to rule were two very different places. Before the war the Czechs had had a parliamentary democracy—the only one in Eastern Europe. The Czech people had enjoyed freedom of speech, freedom of the press and a full range of civil liberties. There had been in Czechoslovakia none of the social tensions which seemed to exist everywhere else. The peasants farmed their own lands; industrial workers were members of strong and influential trade unions, and the rich were nowhere near as rich as they were anywhere else in Europe. But the seeds of destruction of the democratic process were there for all to see. In 1938 the backbone of the nation had been broken by the Munich settlement, in which the parliamentary democracies of Great Britain and France had simply handed Czechoslovakia to Germany on a plate. Very few Czechs were prepared to forgive that betrayal, but only the Communists had a place to go—the Soviet Union.

When the Red Army liberated Prague after the war, it

was to Russia that an increasingly large section of the Czech people looked for guidance and protection. Why should they look to the West, which had sold them out so cynically to the Fascists? What was so noble about the concept of democracy, when the democracies themselves had treated them so ignobly? As a result, in completely free elections in 1946, the Communists had polled 38 percent of the votes and became the strongest single party in the Czech parliament.

That same year Gottwald became prime minister, and in 1948 he destroyed the proud democratic framework of the Czechoslovakian republic by a bloodless coup which established the country once and for all as a Communist state. He had done it not to seize power (which he had achieved as prime minister), but because, as a committed Communist, he saw as a dangerous pipedream the vain notion of the old democratic politicians that Czechoslovakia could become a bridge between East and West. Czechoslovakia, like every other country in Europe, had to choose sides or become, as it had been before the war, merely a staging area for one of the great powers to seize on the way to a full-scale global war. Gottwald chose the side of Russia, convinced that by so doing he was ensuring the independence of his country. The applied politics of geography persuaded many non-Communist Czechs to agree with him.

Klement Gottwald took over the presidency with high hopes. He was shrewd and experienced enough to know that Joseph Stalin would be a rapacious and demanding ally, but he believed that he could handle him, and for a time he did. Because of Gottwald's great skill as a political maneuverer, Operation Splinter Factor had pretty well failed, too—and in the one country in Europe where success had always seemed preordained. If there were any doubts in Washington that the Hungarians or the Poles could ever be persuaded to revolt, there were none about the Czechs. With no Red Army units on their soil, proud of their traditions, accustomed to a Western standard of living, the Czechs seemed, at almost any point since the Communist takeover, ready and able to rise up and over-throw the government that most of them regarded as ille-gal. Gottwald and his tough and able right-hand man, Rudolf Slansky, knew this too, and cracked down hard on any signs of incipient revolt.

It was the middle class who took the brunt of what Slansky described as the "sharp course." As far as the lead-ership was concerned, the middle classes had not reacted particularly well to the *Putsch*. Many had fled the country and were working actively against the Czech government from abroad. Officers had been discovered handing over state secrets to Western diplomats. (Treason had lost all meaning as a crime when it was widely believed that the government itself was a treasonable conspiracy.) As an indication of how serious the situation was, the minister of social welfare announced three months after the coup d'état that 8,300 people had been "purged," a figure which excluded those who had fled abroad. His records showed that in fact over 9,500 were dismissed: 5,800 had previously been employed in nationalized and privately owned con-cerns and 2,500 were civil servants; another 1,432 had been shifted to new positions. Most of those who lost their jobs during that period were men and women incapable of accepting the new Communist regime which had suddenly come to power.

By July 1948, six months after the coup, the middle classes had had enough and staged the largest and most effective anti-Communist demonstration yet seen in any Communist country.

To anyone but a Czech, the setting was peculiar. During the second half of the nineteenth century, an organization formed to promote physical culture became the rallying symbol for Czech nationalism against the old Hapsburg monarchy. It was known as Sokol-Falcon, and the Falcons soon became not only a mass organization but, during the First Republic (1918–1938), a nationalistic political movement which had an influence out of proportion to its ordained purpose. Its officers tended to be on the right of Czech politics and its members belonged largely to the middle classes. Though the Communists had, before the war, sought to establish a rival organization, the Falcons were so deeply entrenched that even after the *Putsch* it was unthinkable that their annual week-long congress in Prague should not be held as usual or that the president of the republic should not take the salute during the great march.

The parade of some 4,000 athletes quickly turned into a major anti-government demonstration. From seemingly nowhere, American, British and, perhaps most significantly of all, Yugoslav flags appeared in the hands of many of the marchers. Cheers were raised for former President Benes and Marshal Tito. Many of the Falcons turned their heads away in a gesture of contempt as they marched past Gottwald's saluting base.

Three months later, the Falcons staged an even more impressive demonstration, this time at the funeral of Social Democrat Benes. Only recent access to internal Czech files indicates how imminent a counterrevolution actually was. The Falcons decided that the funeral should not be conducted by his Communist successors, and literally thousands of people tried to get into Prague and physically take over the funeral from the state authorities. Had they succeeded, the spark of counterrevolution could not have been quenched. But the police managed to keep the demonstrators at bay and the funeral went off as planned.

Rudolf Slansky, the party's first secretary, told the Praesidium of the Central Committee on September 9, two days after the funeral:

> . . the reactionaries wanted to exploit the funeral as an excuse for provocations in a grandiose manner, in order to achieve what they failed to achieve in February. It became an anti-government demonstration. It would have included some 100,000 people, and in spite of the published warnings an enormous number did come to Prague. We correctly described this affair as an attempt at a *Putsch*. That is precisely what it turned out to be. The reactionaries wanted to gain control of the streets. Leaflets exhorting people to an open fight, to occupation of the ministries, railway stations, post offices, etc., were published.

It had been the most remarkable demonstration yet against Communist power in Eastern Europe. The opposition, victims of their own and American propaganda that all Czechs were anti-government, believed that once they showed the lead, the people would rise spontaneously with them and throw off the shackles of Moscow. But, as the postwar elections had shown, the average factory worker was a committed Communist prepared to believe that all the faults of the economy which were biting them so hard were the result not of too much communism but of too little.

As it was, the countercoup failed and Slansky drew the appropriate lessons: " . . . the workers demand strong steps to be taken against the reactionaries," he said. "In my opinion, it is high time to take action against the reactionaries. . . . A law for the protection of the republic will be accepted by the government. .... This is good but ... I recommend that we pass a law on forced labor camps." Not everyone at that secret meeting agreed with their first secretary, but, in the months that followed, Slansky's lash was to be felt with increasing ferocity on the backs of the Czech people.

Gottwald, less severe, clung to the belief that socialism did not necessarily mean a police state, political prisoners and the full paraphernalia of show trials, and he persuaded Slansky to follow a more moderate line. And because of his early courageous stand, Splinter Factor's primary target, Czechoslovakia, managed to emerge remarkably unscathed from the upheavals which the operation caused in her neighboring countries.

Yet Allen Dulles and his colleagues continued to believe that if a counterrevolution could be stirred up anywhere it would be in Czechoslovakia. Most of the members of the party and the government lacked the complete ruthlessness of Communist leaders elsewhere, and that weakness, as Dulles characterized this attitude, could be exploited. The involvement of Noel and Hermann Field made Czechoslovakia an even more natural target. Between them they had a formidable list of friends and contacts in Prague, most of whom held senior positions inside the party and government.

But Dulles had miscalculated. The very traditions which he hoped to exploit gave the Czechs the will to resist. They had not regarded Noel Field as being a particularly dangerous figure, and had had to be persuaded by General Belkin to arrange for his arrest. They had handed him over to the Hungarians with evident reluctance and, less than eager to permit Gejza Pavlik and his wife to be taken to Budapest for interrogation, they had demanded their return. What is more, when Pavlik retracted his confession, which, he said, had been extracted by the Hungarians under torture, the Czechs were inclined to believe him and treated him as kindly as the circumstances permitted. So Dulles sought to tighten the screws.

Colonel Swiatlo, in Poland, was working overtime on the Czech affair. He personally saw the Czech security chief and demanded that members of Field's "criminal gang" inside Czechoslovakia be arrested. He persuaded both President Bierut of Poland and Party Secretary Rakosi of Hungary to exert utmost pressure upon the seemingly reluctant Czech government. But the Czechs still brushed aside every demand for stern action with the formation of yet another commission of inquiry whose findings were always more vague than the one which preceded it. But Czech resistance couldn't last forever.

On September 3, 1949, Rakosi sent President Gottwald a remarkable letter.

> In two weeks, we shall begin the case of the first group of accused in the Rajk trial. The indictment will be published in a week. In this connection we come up against the difficulty that, if we include in this group spies who were sent from England to Hungary, Czechoslovak names will appear by the dozen at the hearing, names which you also know. All these people are at liberty. This part of the hearing would come as a surprise to the Czechoslovak public. One should realize beforehand that in such an eventuality the hard core of the people named would protest vehemently about the things said in court, and this would link them with the Titoists, who, of course, will not spare any effort to undermine the credibility of the charges leveled against them.

Rakosi's list of Czech party officials included the internationally respected Vladimir Clementis, foreign secretary; Vaclav Nosek, minister of the interior; Artur London, deputy foreign minister; Otto Sling, regional party secretary in Slovakia; Eugen Loebl, deputy minister of foreign trade; and Ludvik Rejka, chairman of the National Economic Commission.

To ignore this letter would have put Gottwald and everyone else involved in an invidious position. Nobody believed for a moment that these men were American agents, and yet to pretend that these allegations had never been made could have put into question their own loyalty. Clearly, something had to be done. Some of the people—though none of the big names—on Rakosi's list were hauled in for questioning, but, to the disgust of the Poles and Hungarians, all were exonerated. By the time the Rajk trial began only six people were in prison in Czechoslovakia in connection with the Field case, at least three of whom probably had been under justifiable observation for quite some time.

But Gottwald eventually capitulated, and on September 16, 1949, he and his party secretary, Rudolf Slansky, formally requested the Russians to send in two Soviet advisers on security. Likhachev and Makarov arrived in Prague on September 23. Immediately the atmosphere changed. Nourished by another report from Swiatlo that of the hundred or so people linked with the Fields and under arrest in Poland all had compromised prominent Czechs and that the conspiratorial center for the enemies of the peoples' democracies was to be found in Prague, the two advisers set about their task.

Again Swiatlo tried to stoke up the flames. He told President Bierut that despite all his warnings and those of Hungarian security, the Czechs were deliberately sheltering enemies of the party in their midst. The fact that they had done little or nothing about it must mean that there were men high up in the Czech government protecting spies and saboteurs from the full rigors of the law.

East European countries had noticed, too, that the Czechs were still doing a surprising amount of trade with the West. No one was prepared to acknowledge that the Czech ministers were in a very difficult position. Since Czechoslovakia was by far the most industrially advanced country in the bloc, having had extensive economic relations with the West for many years, it was clearly impossible to dismantle these overnight without having a very serious effect upon the Czech economy as a whole.

Though they tried to defend themselves, the Czechs came under heavy criticism. Inferences of economic sabotage lay heavy in the air. The Czechs did everything possible to come to terms with their colleagues, and at a Comecon Council meeting, though still facing criticisms, they were gratified to hear Anastas Mikoyan's report that the Czech comrades were now aware of the needs of reorientating their production to the needs of other socialist countries.

The effect of this "reorientation" was to drive the Czech standard of living down still further and put the government and party under renewed pressure at home. Rudolf Slansky was quick to draw the fire away from the government and look for a scapegoat elsewhere: "Our people have great patience," he said. "When one examines certain economic defects ... one sees that an enemy is behind it."

All of this was to have a profound effect upon President Gottwald. Where only a few months earlier he was prepared to resist outside pressure, now he was prepared to listen to any charge, however outrageous. The truth is that between May and December 1949 his health had deteriorated to such an extent that he no longer either controlled or even knew what was going on.

A perfect illustration of Gottwald's vulnerability can be found in the case of Vladimir Clementis, the gentle and likable Czech foreign minister of world repute, who had been marked down early by the Splinter Factor team as an easy target. The initial purpose, in fact, was not to create around him a show trial, as in the case of Rajk, but to persuade him to defect to the West, thus providing a massive propaganda boost for the West and throwing immense suspicion on all of his associates and friends.

There was an additional bonus to be had as well. Clementis was Slovak, and already there were signs that the Slovak people were becoming increasingly restive as the country moved from crisis to crisis. Chafing under Czech rule from Prague, Slovak nationalism began to reexert itself again, and many Slovaks began to look to Clementis for a lead. If Allen Dulles could help cause an irreparable rift between the Czech lands and Slovakia, then nothing could serve the cause of the Western democracies better. So Clementis became the next target.

But before Clementis could be dealt with, Otto Sling, the Slovak regional party secretary, had to be got out of the way. He had joined the party at the age of twenty-two, fought in the Spanish civil war and spent the years of World War II as an *émigré* in England. A tough, no-nonsense Stalinist who liked to organize his own local show trials and who regarded prison as the ideal environment for his critics, he was rapidly becoming a power in the land. Thought of as a future first secretary of the party (a rival to Slansky) and even one day president, Sling managed at the same time to be a repressive autocrat and a man who increased production and efficiency within his bailiwick.

Impatient, disinclined to listen to anyone, he made as many mistakes as enemies. Considered by many as being too rigid, he was equally criticized for failing to appoint prewar Communists to senior positions and for "slackness in applying Soviet experience." Ironically, the security apparatus decided to use against Sling the very weapons which they were encouraging in Prague: they accused him of illegal procedures in the arrest, interrogation and subsequent trials of party members. Various commissions sat to decide whether Sling had been guilty of dictatorial methods and illegal persecutions of long-serving party members. For once, however, the security people were outwitted by the politicians, who had little desire to crucify a colleague on charges which subsequently could be used against them.

Sling, in fact, nearly escaped altogether. A special party commission convened to review what was known as the Brno affair. Although the commission had produced a draft of a resolution for discussion by the Central Committee concerning "errors in methods of words in the conduct of cadre policy by the Brno Regional Committee" of the party, it nevertheless suggested no disciplinary measures, in a way confirming Sling in the rightness of his course. It was a major blow, for without Sling, it would be impossible to proceed against Clementis. No one in Czechoslovakia would believe the line that Clementis was the leader of a Slovak anti-state center without Sling being involved too.

However, a new Soviet security adviser, Vladimir Boyarsky, came up with the answer and destroyed both Sling and Clementis. Through him a Czech security officer "discovered" a letter written by Sling to an officer in Czech military intelligence before the war. It was a simple communication to an intelligence officer, Emanuel Voska, on April 17, 1939, offering assistance of an unspecified nature. Taken into conjunction with all of the other charges leveled against Sling, it was the one piece of evidence which gave a coherent pattern to all his activities in the past. Where previously his policies appeared mistaken, they could now be regarded as treasonable.

Boyarsky demanded immediate action; President Gottwald presented it to the Praesidium, and on October 6, 1950, Sling was arrested.* Under the most terrible tortures, Sling confessed to espionage. On November 10 and 11 a regional party committee expelled Sling from the party, describing him, at the suggestion of President Gottwald himself, as "an enemy agent."

On the night of November 11 the big roundup began: friends and associates of Sling were herded into prisons throughout the region and accused of what came to be called "Slingism." Wherever Sling had been the authorities now found enemies of the party. No sector of society escaped, not even the security services itself. Leading military men—such as General Bulander, chief of the military staff in the office of the president of the republic, and General Zdenek Novak, army commander of the Third Military Region—were arrested. But even that did not satisfy Boyarsky. Sling's protectors were still at large, he said, and they must be in the top echelons of the party hierarchy. And so began a purge of the purgers.

Accompanying all of this was one of the most extraordinary propaganda campaigns ever launched by a nation at peace against one of its own citizens. The daily papers throughout Czechoslovakia devoted 2,971,000 lines of newsprint to the exposure of Sling and his criminal clique. Every adult in the republic was sent a copy of a brochure containing a speech by President Gottwald denouncing Sling and all his works.

Meanwhile the CIA had been working on the Clementis case. In October 1949 Clementis attended the U.N. General Assembly in New York, and immediately a two-pronged attack, designed to persuade him to seek political

---

* Some authorities, such as Artur London in *On Trial*, say that Sling was arrested in November. However, I believe that he was arrested on October 6 and that his arrest was kept secret for some time. Even Czech official records are unclear about the exact date.

asylum, was launched by the CIA through its State Department outlets and by SIS through the Foreign Office. Journalists were told by senior officials that Clementis was one of the few independently minded politicians of Eastern Europe: he was "fighting against the increasing Stalinist grip upon Czechoslovakia"; he was "opposed to men like Gottwald." Talks which Clementis had with Western statesmen were sufficiently distorted in their presentation to journalists that he was made to appear almost virulently anti-Soviet.

Totally confused by what was going on, Clementis was forced to telephone Gottwald almost daily to deny yet another statement being attributed to him and apologize for the quite extraordinary impression which he seemed to be making.

Then came stage two of the plot. This time a story appeared in a Swiss newspaper which claimed that Clementis would be arrested as soon as he got back to Prague. It was Gottwald, who really had no intention of doing anything of the kind, whose turn it was to telephone Clementis and deny the truth of this story. As a mark of his trust in Clementis, he sent Clementis's wife, Ludmilla, to New York, carrying a personal message assuring his great and good friend of his total admiration and support. The presence of Ludmilla Clementis in New York forced the CIA to make a direct approach to Clementis, but he, essentially a political innocent, brushed aside the invitation to defect, and returned to Prague.

Gottwald had no knowledge of how far the case against Clementis had gone since the Slovak was first denounced by Rakosi as a member of the Field conspiracy. Clementis himself was to know as soon as he arrived back in Prague. On March 13, 1950, he was called to Hradcany Castle, the presidential palace, and dismissed by Gottwald.

He was arrested ten months later, at the end of January 1951.

By that time, the Slovak purge had spread like a dark virus throughout the country. Already an unbelievable 169,000 card-carrying members of the Czechoslovakian Communist party had been arrested—10 percent of the entire membership. It was one of the greatest political purges of all time. And of the 169,000, well over half were Slovaks, and they were accused of a new crime: bourgeois Slovak nationalism.

In the meantime, news came from Jozef Swiatlo that Marie Svermova had been named by Hermann Field as a contact, and so she too was locked away in prison. The shock to Slovakia was, if anything, greater than when Sling was arrested, for Svermova was the widow of the revered national hero, Jan Sverma, who was killed in the Slovak uprising, and the sister of Karel Svab, deputy minister of the interior and head of security. It had gone that high.

On January 28, 1951, about the same time that Clementis was arrested, Artur London was snatched away from his wife and children. Despite resisting heroically, Sling had finally confessed to everything, and after months in prison he was too broken a man to recant. He implicated almost everybody—but principally London and Clementis.

The whole country began to disintegrate under this political pressure. In February 1951 rationing coupons for bread, pastry and flour were reintroduced and the prices of these goods were increased. The cost of manufactured goods became prohibitive. With salaries at about 5,000 korunas a month, a very ordinary radio cost 15,000 korunas. At the end of November, the revered custom of Christmas bonuses was scrapped and rations were cut again.

Clearly, the leadership hoped that the Sling/Svermova/Clementis revelations would take some of the heat off the shortcomings of the economy. But only the really dedicated party workers were taken in.

By the summer of 1951 the situation had become explosive. Strikes broke out almost everywhere, including Prague itself. Large factories in Brno stopped work, and thousands of workers took to demonstrating in the streets. Protest delegations from various districts converged on Prague and violently disrupted public and party meetings. Eventually, even party functionaries in the regions joined the protest, and delegations to Prague included district secretaries and members of the local praesidiums.

It was a revolutionary situation, exactly what Splinter Factor had been designed for. But by now it was running under its own steam—there was no need for *agents provocateurs*. Free Czech forces stationed with the American army's own International Brigade in Nuremberg, Germany, were put on the alert to assist a spontaneous uprising in Czechoslovakia, which was expected any minute. And still it didn't come.

It had been so close that one more push seemed justified, one more stroke so audacious that the entire governmental and party structure in Prague would have to disintegrate. Splinter Factor had lost all interest in the now-imprisoned Vladimir Clementis. Allen Dulles was after the biggest catch of all.

Chapter 13

The Great Crossing Sweeper

Rudolf Slansky was the second most powerful man in Czechoslovakia. Indeed, by 1950, with Gottwald withdrawing more and more into himself, Slansky virtually ran the party and the country. Power sat easily upon the shoulders of this man, who, though slightly colorless in public, was always respected and often feared. He was an out-and-out Stalinist whose actions matched his words. The opposition had to be crushed by force; the enemy had to be rooted out and exterminated. Better that ten innocents suffer than one guilty man go free.

To Allen Dulles and the CIA, Rudolf Slansky was the one man capable of keeping Czechoslovakia inside the Communist bloc. Only he was able to control the simmering revolt. Slansky had to go. He was to be removed by the same methods which Dulles had ruthlessly used on so many others.

The son of a wealthy merchant, with a powerful build, red hair and beetled eyebrows, Slansky was an imposing man. He had thrown himself into the party's work from his earliest days. Though the Communist party was a legal party in Czechoslovakia, it was in constant trouble with the police for illegal activities in fomenting strikes and general discontent.

Though Slansky could have easily and honorably remained a respectable front man for the party, he chose the more dangerous and infinitely less comfortable role of a party activist in the field; by 1936, on the run from the police, he had to leave the country for the Soviet Union. Then, during the war, Slansky again showed that he was not wanting for courage. As one of the leaders of the party, he had an important role to play in Moscow, but he decided to parachute into Slovakia to fight with the Slovakian partisans against the Germans. It wasn't, by the standards of the Second World War, a big war. And yet it was as heroic as any; hundreds died in the icy and treacherous mountains of Slovakia.

But those who knew Slansky well—and in the early days he was a popular and amusing companion—say that it was the very mysterious kidnapping of his youngest child in Moscow during the war that changed him, gave him that quality of withdrawal, toughened and probably coarsened him.

However, those who suffered at his hands after the war could not be expected to make these allowances for him. All they knew was that he had become the purger of the nation, a man with seemingly no humanity or pity. The Americans had no doubt either that Slansky deserved no other fate than the one they had in mind.

The best secret operation requires a little bit of luck, and Allen Dulles had that luck then. General Gehlen was able to produce a German agent—a Czech Swiatlo—who

was firmly entrenched in the upper rungs of the Czech
security apparatus. Although the identity of this agent is
still not known today, there is no doubt that he existed; in
fact, he was so much in control that at one stage of the
operation he even deliberately ignored the direct orders of
Marshal Stalin.

It was also a bonus that the Czech Fieldists mentioned Rudolf Slansky early on in their interrogations.
After all, it was Slansky who had appointed them to their
posts and had given them their orders. Many of the prisoners mentioned him, as well as President Gottwald, to indicate how farcical were the charges being laid against them.
If they could show that the policies which they had advocated, and which were later suspect, were not theirs but
Slansky's, then, they reasoned, their innocence would be
established.

Up to the middle of the summer of 1951 it was the
intention of the government to hold a show trial featuring
Otto Sling, the Czech Rajk, as the main defendant. In
February 1951 a security commission gave the Central
Committee a full description of Sling and his crimes. He
was a "spy, brute, cynic and murderer"; he was also a
"criminal monster, a vicious pervert" and "a wicked adven-
turer." His plan had been to kill both Gottwald and Slansky and seize the leadership. But as the name of Rudolf
Slansky emerged more and more in the interrogations of
both Sling and others, security began looking at the record
of its general secretary with interest. Sling realized that if
he could divert attention from himself, he might escape
with his neck. Deliberately, he began incriminating Slansky. President Gottwald himself, when informed of the line
the questioning of the suspects was taking, expressly for-
bade Slansky's name to be brought up by the interrogator.
But this did not stop the security men.

At this precise point in time Operation Splinter Factor

intervened. Two top security men, Major Smola and Vladimir Kahoutek, jointly decided that the information they had in their possession was too important to ignore and that it had to be made available in the appropriate quarters. So in June of 1951 they persuaded fellow security workers to take the report of the interrogations not to President Gottwald or even to the Soviet advisers, but directly to the Russian ambassador in Prague. It was an incredible act of disloyalty to the sovereign state of Czechoslovakia. It was also a direct invitation to Stalin to intervene. When they heard about this, the Czech party leaders were naturally furious, and at least one of the security men who had gone to the embassy was arrested. But the damage had been done, and Smola and Kahoutek knew it.

So the pressure was kept up. A report, carefully edited by Soviet advisers, concerning security's findings on "Jewish bourgeois nationalism" implicating Slansky and mentioning also Bedrich Geminder, the head of the International Department of the Central Committee, was handed to President Gottwald and the minister of national security, Ladislav Kopriva. Gottwald, under pressure from Kopriva, agreed that questioning on these lines should be permitted and the facts brought to light, but he did not lift the ban he had earlier placed on direct questioning concerning Rudolf Slansky. In other words, if prisoners spoke about Slansky, their statements could be recorded; but they were not to be asked about him. Considering what was going on in the prisons of Czechoslovakia, it was a futile condition.

In July Stalin intervened. The Soviet ambassador in Prague had dutifully notified Stalin about the suspicion concerning Slansky. Perhaps beginning to glimpse the outlines of an American intelligence operation behind the great show trials, Stalin wrote Gottwald a coded letter on the twentieth of the month. "We have received incriminating material about Comrades Slansky and Geminder," he said. "We consider this material insufficient and that there is no cause for making accusations. From this it is evident that there has not been a sufficiently serious attitude to the work being done in Prague, and we have therefore decided to recall Boyarsky [the chief Soviet adviser] to Moscow."

Gottwald acknowledged the letter on the same day. "I agree with you entirely," he said, "that, on the basis of the investigation material, it is not possible to bring any charges against the mentioned comrades and even less to draw any conclusions. This is doubly valid since the statements came from convicted criminals. This was my first impression from the moment I heard about the matter."

Stalin invited Gottwald to Moscow for immediate discussions. But the Czech president excused himself on the grounds of ill health and sent Deputy Prime Minister Alexei Cepicka, his confidential aide, for a full meeting of the Russian Politburo on July 23, where the whole question was thoroughly discussed. Cepicka told the Politburo how the investigation was progressing and how Slansky's and Geminder's names had emerged.

Stalin again sprang to their defense. "This could be a provocation," he said, "on the part of the enemy," and he gave examples of how "honorable members of the party were falsely accused by people who were arrested. If the work of the investigating organs is not to be turned to the benefit of the enemy, it is necessary to exercise constant and rigid control over them and not to allow general mistrust to spread to the highest organs." He had seen through Operation Splinter Factor in a flash of intuition, but he still didn't realize the operation existed.

He sent Cepicka back with a letter to Gottwald: "We think, as before, that the statements of convicted persons, without proof to support them, cannot serve as a basis for the accusations of workers who are known in the party for their positive work. Therefore, you are correct in being careful and in not trusting the statements of experienced malefactors as far as Comrades Slansky and Geminder are concerned."

But Slansky did not get a completely clean slate. Stalin recommended that he be removed from the general secretaryship because he had committed errors by giving senior jobs to "hostile elements." Again, Stalin was right: Slansky had become too autocratic a secretary-general, and unquestionably, from the party's point of view, many of his appointments made against the advice of others had been mistaken. The party was not running smoothly, nor was the government, and Slansky shared a large measure of the responsibility for this. Gottwald instantly agreed to "the organizational measures you advise in the matter of Comrade Slansky. . . . We intend to give him a post in the government [as distinct from the party position he held]."

Interestingly, Gottwald betrayed his real state of mind in a draft of a reply which was never sent. In it he vouched entirely for Slansky and criticized himself. It showed that he was weak and indecisive. Slansky was his closest friend inside the party hierarchy, and yet almost when invited to do so by Stalin himself, Gottwald felt that prudence did not permit him to write in his friend's defense.

A few days later, all of Czechoslovakia celebrated Slansky's fiftieth birthday. Newspapers that day carried articles and letters singing his praises. He was awarded Czechoslovakia's highest decoration, the Order of Klement Gottwald for the Building of Socialism, and most important of all, though this he did not know, the minister of the interior sent a directive to the investigators, quoting both Stalin and Gottwald, forbidding any more direct questioning concerning Slansky.

In September 1951 Slansky lost his powerful position as party secretary but still remained a member of the Politburo, as deputy prime minister. The Central Committee, in accepting Slansky's self-criticism, said he "admitted his mistakes with Bolshevik frankness."*

News of Slansky's demotion was met with delight throughout the country. Those hostile to the party, who had regarded him with fear, and for good reason, felt that the dismissal of the country's most prominent hard-liner must mean a relaxation of the whole terror machine which he had constructed. Party members, among whom he had never been particularly popular, were equally fervent in their acclamation. It was clear to even the most fanatical that a Communist government had not proved quite the blessing they had expected. The economy was reeling from one crisis to the next. The average worker was sullen and hostile. Now that the top leadership was acknowledging that mistakes had been made and removing from office the man who was responsible for them, a wave of hope spread through the country—and Gottwald's prestige rose still further. Everyone knew that Slansky had been his friend and close colleague for over twenty years. Yet friendship was not being permitted to stand in the way of honest government.

To Allen Dulles, Stalin's uncharacteristic intervention had interfered with an operation which was running very nicely. Admittedly, he hadn't stopped it, for the security men involved, including principally Allen Dulles's German agent, simply ignored the order and continued asking their prisoners about Slansky.

* The fascinating Stalin-Gottwald correspondence appears in *The Czechoslovak Political Trials, 1950–1954* (London: Macdonald and Company, 1971), an edited version by Jiri Pelikan of the 1968 Czech Governmental Commission Report on the purge trials, which was suppressed before it could be published in Prague.

In August, a month before Slansky had been demoted, they felt they had enough "evidence" against him to admit that they had disobeyed orders. They had extracted a statement from Karel Svab, the ex-chief of security and deputy minister of the interior, who was in prison for some months, to the effect that Slansky was guilty of espionage and subversion. President Gottwald took this report seriously enough to agree that he no longer had any objections to direct interrogations concerning Slansky.

If Dulles's hopes were raised again, they were dashed completely when the government reorganization was announced, and Slansky's new position, still one of power, became clear. Certainly Splinter Factor's Polish operation was not working as well as it should. Gomulka had been arrested by Swiatlo in August 1951, though there seemed to be no guarantee that he ever would be brought to trial. But at least he had been imprisoned. By contrast, the Czech operation was working catastrophically. By taking the incriminating evidence against Slansky directly to the Russian embassy, the operation had merely awakened in Stalin's mind the suspicion that he was the victim of a hoax. Although Slansky had been humiliated, his demotion had strengthened the grip of the party in Czechoslovakia rather than weakened it. Stalin had proved that he was in no mood to condemn Slansky out of hand, and it was doubtful if more evidence of the same caliber would persuade him to change his mind. Gottwald was by now weak enough to succumb to the slightest pressure from his security people and was prepared to sacrifice his old friend, but he certainly could not be relied upon to hound him, to initiate action and to persuade Stalin that Slansky should go down. The prospects looked bleak.

Splinter Factor had worked so well previously because the simple act of denunciation had proved sufficient to

destroy men against whom a political doubt existed. In
Czechoslovakia the security workers were alleging that
Slansky was the head of a conspiracy designed to overthrow the state. The politicians claimed that Sling was the
head of a conspiracy to assassinate Slansky.

There was no question that political grounds—the fact
that Slansky was a Jew—existed for his arrest. Zionism
had suddenly become, at Stalin's behest, as grave a sin as
Titoism, and a Jew in a prominent position once labeled a
Zionist was instantly suspect. Czech Jews were particularly vulnerable. The Communist bloc had initially supported the creation of the State of Israel, an attitude
which was to change as American influence increased in
Israel. Czechoslovakia, however, had supported the Israelis
more vociferously than any other country inside the bloc
—politically, militarily and economically—and perhaps was
a little late in discerning the Kremlin's switch in policy.
The crime of Jewish bourgeois nationalism and Zionism
was already being given an obscene twist inside Ruzyn
prison. In his book *On Trial*, Artur London has testified
how Major Smola seized him by the throat and screamed:
"We'll get rid of you and your filthy race. You're all the
same. Not everything Hitler did was right, but he
destroyed the Jews, and he was right about that. Too
many of you escaped the gas chamber. We'll finish what he
started. We'll bury you and your filthy race ten yards
deep."

By the end of September, a fortnight after Slansky
had been appointed deputy premier, Allen Dulles decided
that the exercise was in such danger that a rescue operation
had to be mounted immediately. The plan was ready by
the end of October and fully operational at the beginning
of November. Not since the earliest days of Operation
Splinter Factor, when the Fields were being set up as

American agents, did the CIA have to use "direct action" —the actual planting of incriminating evidence. But now, with Allen Dulles firmly inside the CIA, striking out for the topmost rung,* it was agreed that Rudolf Slansky should become the target of a direct attack, many details of which are still obscure, but which had as its theme the complete destruction of the political and moral credibility of one of the most significant figures in Eastern Europe.

Like the best of political intelligence operations, it began with a rumor. Czech *émigrés*, especially those in Germany, began to hear whispers at the beginning of November 1951 that Rudolf Slansky, shaken by his demotion, was talking about defecting to the West. Few believed it, but it was something to talk about—a new tidbit to discuss, a lead into yet another debate on the state of the nation since the Communist takeover.

On November 4 the man the Russians believed they had planted inside the CIA Czech operation in Munich, Otto Haupter,† informed the Soviets that arrangements were far enough advanced to lift Rudolf Slansky to the West. Haupter, a Czech Jew, had been arrested in Prague two years previously for espionage. He was a senior American agent and appeared to agree, in exchange for his life and the lives of his family, to work for the Russians if released. Convinced that he would cooperate, the Soviets let Haupter out—the story was that he had escaped—and permitted him to make his way back to Munich to rejoin the Americans. But as soon as he arrived, he told his superior everything. Now he was to be used against the Russians.

On November 9, 1951, he "managed" to pass a message to the Russians about CIA plans to lift Rudolf Slansky to the West. The Russians, who, of course, had heard the pre-

---

* Dulles became director of the CIA on January 7, 1953.
† Otto Haupter is a fictitious name.

vious "rumors," immediately passed the message to Stalin. Haupter told the Russians that he himself was in charge of the Czech end of the operation and would be using his old network. A courier would be crossing the border on the night of November 9 with letters setting up the deal.

Stalin acted promptly, and on November 11 Anastas Mikoyan was in Prague as Stalin's personal representative. He informed President Gottwald that Stalin insisted Slansky be arrested immediately because he was about to escape to the West. This time Gottwald demurred. He told Mikoyan that he had known Slansky for a great many years and he was quite certain that, whatever else he might do, he would not actively go over to the enemy. Mikoyan, returning to the Soviet embassy, spoke to Stalin on the telephone and expressed Gottwald's point of view. Stalin again hesitated—it was as if even now he were reluctant to believe that Slansky really was a traitor. Mikoyan came back to Gottwald, who had been joined by Alexei Cepicka, the deputy prime minister, and told him that the only reason Stalin had for requesting his arrest was that he had heard that Slansky might try to leave the country. Gottwald agreed that Stalin must have "serious reasons" to believe such a thing, but felt more evidence was necessary.

In the meantime, Haupter sent the letters to his contact in Czechoslovakia, Daniela Kankovska, setting up a meeting the following week. As hoped, a Soviet agent had them copied and resealed. They reached Kankovska on November 14, but fortunately she sensed that something was seriously wrong and destroyed them. It was another close shave for Splinter Factor. If the Soviets had relied upon finding the letters in Kankovska's possession and had not intercepted them, the operation would have foundered again. But they were cleverer than that.

Already, on November 9, Czech radio monitors had

picked up on Radio Free Europe transmission a reading: "Bad things are coming to light, says Ceston." By the time the letters were in the hands of Russian and Czech security officers that message began to make some sense.

The letters were addressed, picturesquely, to "The Great Crossing Sweeper." They referred to Gomulka's fate in Poland, and offered Slansky safe transportation across the frontier and a job, though outside politics, in the West. They provided contacts in Czechoslovakia who would help as well as coded messages from "Ceston" over the Radio Free Europe transmitter, the first of which had already been broadcast on November 10. The next broadcasts were scheduled for November 17, November 24 and December 1. Munich was by now abuzz with rumors, all faithfully reported back to Moscow. To help them along, a peculiar piece of theater was reenacted for a week at the American military airfield. Prominent Czech *émigrés* were taken there every night to await "an important arrival." They were not told, as they stood with senior American officers at the end of the runway night after night, who the "important arrival" was to be. But they all guessed: Rudolf Slansky. Though they were all pledged to secrecy about their futile vigil, the news got out very quickly. Charles Katek, head of the CIA operation in Munich and former U.S. military attaché in Prague, made sure of that. From now on, there was no doubt in Moscow or Prague as to what had to be done.

So on November 23, 1951, President Gottwald called in Prime Minister Zapotocky, Minister of National Security Kopriva and the Soviet security adviser, Alexei Beschasnov. Gottwald somberly told them of the evidence which had now been collected about Rudolf Slansky and ordered his arrest that night.

Zapotocky flushed. "He's having dinner at my home

this evening," he said, clearly embarrassed. "I will have to cancel him."

It was Beschasnov who put a stop to that. "There is evidence," he said, "that he may be trying to leave the country. Everything must progress as normal. He must not be put on his guard." In a way, he was doing Rudolf Slansky a favor. The Great Crossing Sweeper was being permitted one last splendid meal which suited his rank and station.

Chapter 14

A Sackful of Ashes

It had been a cordial and pleasant evening. The host was the prime minister of Czechoslovakia, Antonin Zapotocky. The chief guests were a group of Soviet economic advisers returning the following day to Moscow after a tour of duty in Czechoslovakia. The party at the prime minister's villa residence was small and select: the prime minister and his wife; Anatoli Laurentjev, the new Soviet ambassador; Viliam Siroky, the minister of foreign affairs; Gustav Kliment, the minister of heavy industry; Jaromir Dolansky, the minister of the State Planning Office, and his wife; and finally the deputy premier, Rudolf Slansky, and his wife, Josefa.

The date was November 23, 1951—Klement Gottwald's birthday—and the assembled company drank his health and also Joseph Stalin's. The Slanskys, who normally on these occasions called on the president to offer their congratulations, were told that he was too ill to see anyone. So they sent him a painting of his native village instead.

Just after midnight, Josefa Slanska, worrying about her husband's health—he was suffering from a liver ailment—suggested they go home. The prime minister's wife telephoned for a car, and the Slanskys, after saying warm goodbyes, left.

Their villa was in darkness when they arrived. Mrs. Slanska stumbled, and Rudolf angrily told his guards to find out what had happend to the lights. He opened the front door and stepped into the pitch-black hall, and then the lights went on. Mrs. Slanska's arm was twisted behind her back. Rudolf Slansky had been seized by two men who were holding him by the kitchen door. Other men with automatic machine pistols were ranged along the walls, braced, ready to fire if anyone made a run for it. Josefa screamed (an "inhuman howl" is how she described it in her book, *Report on My Husband*), and a hand was clamped across her mouth to keep her quiet. She was driven to a deserted hut in the forest near Prague, where she was joined by her sixteen-year-old son, Rudi. Her daughter, Maria, was taken to a children's home. Rudolf Slansky was driven to Ruzyn prison.

The man who only a few months ago had been the second most powerful man in Czechoslovakia and who, on his fiftieth birthday three months earlier, was told by Gottwald: ". . . our whole party, our whole working people salutes you as its faithful son and warrior, filled with love for the working classes and with loyalty to the Soviet Union and to great Stalin"—this man was now being arraigned as a traitor and a spy.

They chained him like a dog, kept him in a straitjacket and beat him again and again. Interrogations continued around the clock. For over a month Slansky refused to confess anything except political errors, for which he had already criticized himself at the Central Committee meeting in September.

He wrote a letter to the Praesidium of the party:

> I am aware of the fact that my arrest must have been due to serious—though to me unknown—reasons, but as far as the suspicion against me, a suspicion that I committed some crimes against the party, is concerned, this must be due to some horrible mistake. Never in my life did I betray the party or damage it knowingly—never did I make pacts with the enemy.
>
> May I ask you one favor: do not pass on me, in advance, a judgment as if I were an enemy. I am not an enemy. I am firmly convinced that the accusations against me will be proved false.

But soon he knew that the hope was false. For wasn't he the man who had driven so many others down this same road?

He could resist no longer. Several times his suffering exceeded the limits of endurance and he lost consciousness for hours on end. Once, trying to commit suicide, he asked an interrogator if he could go to the lavatory. The interrogator left the room for a moment to call the guard, and Slansky leapt after him and locked the door. Frantically, and in vain, he searched for the interrogator's service pistol and then tried to hang himself from a noose he fashioned out of a cord from one of the window sashes. By the time the door was broken down he was unconscious, but he was brought back to life with injections and artificial respiration. The doctor who performed this service was later honored.

The interrogations went on into summer. Hundreds of people, high and low, throughout the country, were being arrested because they knew Slansky or had been appointed by him. All were invited to contribute to the massive dossier which was being built up against him.

Preparations began for the trial, but there were so many people in prison that it was difficult to decide who would be the main defendants along with him. Once the actors had been chosen, security officers worked out with the accused their roles and helped them learn them by heart. The judges, prosecutors and defense lawyers were prepared too for their parts in the play. Nothing was left to chance. The fear that one of the defendants might choose to "defect" in open court plagued the security men, who remembered the Kostov trial.

So a dress rehearsal was held: the judges, the prosecutors, the defense counsels and the defendants went through their allotted roles. This was tape-recorded, and an elaborate signaling arrangement was then established between the president of the court and a security man, who would be able to indicate to the president the instant one of the defendants strayed from the script so that he could call an instant adjournment.

The leadership did not even bother to pretend to themselves that the trial was to be anything but a farce. For they too went through the transcript before the trial took place, and ordered various changes. Deputy Premier Alexei Cepicka, who had risen to prominence because he had married Gottwald's daughter, thought that "from the legal point the charges [were] weak" and suggested ways of strengthening them. Foreign Minister Viliam Siroky thought that the accused spoke too much and that greater emphasis should be given to the indictment. Gottwald felt it was a mistake to stress their hostile activities inside the party; the party had expelled them already, and they could hardly be charged in a court of law for that.

On November 20, 1952, almost exactly a year after his arrest, Rudolf Slansky and his fellow "conspirators" were put up into the dock in the state court in Prague. The defendants were, to quote the indictment: Rudolf Slansky, of Jewish origin, former central secretary of the Communist party of Czechoslovakia and, at the time of his arrest, deputy prime minister; Bedrich Geminder, of Jewish origin, former director of the International Department of the Communist party's Central Committee; Ludvik Frejka, of Jewish origin, former head of the national-economic section of the Office of the President of the Republic; Josef Frank, Czech, former deputy to the central secretary of the Communist party of Czechoslovakia; Vladimir Clementis, Slovak, former minister of foreign affairs; Bedrich Reicin, of Jewish origin, former deputy to the national minister of defense; Karel Svab, Czech, former deputy to the minister of national security; Artur London, of Jewish origin, former deputy to the minister of foreign affairs; Vavro Hajdu, of Jewish origin, former deputy to the minister of foreign affairs; Eugen Loebl, of Jewish origin, former deputy to the minister of foreign trade; Rudolf Margolius, of Jewish origin, former deputy to the minister of foreign trade; Otto Fischl, of Jewish origin, former deputy to the minister of finance; Otto Sling, of Jewish origin, former leading secretary of the Communist party in Brno; Andrej Simon, of Jewish origin, former editor of *Rude Pravo*. These people all "progressively conspired together, both among themselves and with other persons, in an attempt to destroy the independence of the Republic and the people's democratic organization of the state, which is guaranteed by the constitution; by which means to a remarkable degree, they brought the said state organizations into peril. . . . "

No confession during all of the East European purges was as abject as Slansky's. He pleaded guilty on all four counts: espionage, high treason, sabotage and military treason.

The prosecutor described the background of the case to the court:

> The imperialists, well aware of the strength of the Communist party, began to prepare this agency in the period of the pre-Munich Republic and, giving it a special importance in their plans for the postwar period, reinforced it on the eve of the war. From the end of 1938, in London and afterward in Krakow, under the pretext of helping Czechoslovakians and other refugees, the so-called British Committee, later known as the Trust Fund, was an important Anglo-American espionage agency and acted under the cover of the British Ministry of Home Affairs. Here the agency was selected and trained from the ranks of the refugees and afterward was, with the help of the Trust Fund, sent from Krakow to London. This activity was directed by Hermann Field and later by his brother, Noel Field, both the closest cooperators of Allen Dulles, chief of the U.S. espionage organization OSS, carrying on espionage activities in Central and Eastern Europe.

Slansky, it was alleged, put into positions of authority men he knew to be "Fieldists" in order to establish the conspiratorial center with the aim of overthrowing the government.*

* Even Britain's own little side show, destroying the reputation of left-wing Labour members of parliament with their East European friends, was given its moment of glory. Konni Zilliacus, a British M.P. of great charm and erudition who was far to the left of his party policy, was given a chapter to himself at the trial. He was described by the prosecutor as British intelligence's "well-tried henchman, a master of deceit and provocation . . . one of the most experienced agents in British intelligence." Poor Zilliacus wandered around Westminster for months, a very bemused-looking gentleman. But it got a lot of laughs at 21, Queen Anne's Gate.

The newspapers produced their most colorful prose writers to cover the case. *Rude Pravo*, the official party newspaper, outdid itself. This is how they described Slansky as he gave his evidence:

> The cowardly, treacherous eyes flicker in the mask of wrinkles, against the fall of red hair, and for a fraction of a second peer around the hall. He walks slowly, and sits down on the bench of the accused, and for a moment it seems that he is repentant. . . . He nods his head in time with his "Yes" to the questions of his guilt. . . . Without emotion, in an incomprehensibly and repellently calm voice, he begins to speak of his monstrous crimes, and the sum of them is that this one solitary wretch has committed more evil than hundreds of hardened criminals. . . . The unmasking of Slansky—the arch scoundrel—and his anti-state group has saved our country from ruin, saved it to enjoy a happy life and a safe progress toward socialism and peace.

So the case rolled on to its preordained and tragic conclusion. The sentences came as no surprise. Death to all except Artur London, Vavro Hajdu and Eugen Loebl, who had been in prison since November 24, 1949. They were sentenced to life imprisonment.

None of those sentenced appealed. Pleas for mercy were rejected, and the executions were carried out on December 3, 1952. The eleven who were hanged were each allowed to write last letters to their families. Only Rudolf Slansky knew the score too well to bother. He knew it was all a cruel trick, like so many of the other tricks played upon him and his fellow condemned while they were in prison. He was sure that the letters would never be delivered—as indeed they were not.

Colonel Swiatlo had one last request. He persuaded

President Bierut to write on his behalf, asking Gottwald's permission to interrogate Slansky and the others concerning their contact with Gomulka and Field. Gottwald agreed. Swiatlo made the trip to Prague, but the prisoners could tell him nothing. Gomulka still was able to cling precariously to his life. But not the eleven of Czechoslovakia.

Stalin was not to reign for very much longer; three months later, on March 5, 1953, he was dead. Operation Splinter Factor died with him. Throughout the whole of Eastern Europe, Stalin had left a bloody trail. Yet he was as much a victim of forces greater than he as were those who ended up dancing at the end of a hangman's rope, or those who died because the torturer had gone too far, or those who killed themselves, or those whose hearts gave out in the brutal regime of a labor camp. Hundreds were killed by that deadly combination of Joseph Stalin and Operation Splinter Factor. Many more still were driven insane as they discovered the faith to which they had clung all their lives had been handed over in the night to criminal sadists, who explained that it was necessary to manufacture an entire edifice of lies in order that the party remain strong. Thousands were sent to the camps and were never altogether whole again. Thousands more lost their jobs. Intellectuals who had never wielded anything heavier than a pen found work as laborers on building sites. And even there they were bullied and harassed, paid less than the rate for the job while their foreman pocketed the difference, knowing that they were grateful for any work and dared not complain. No one can say exactly how many people were involved in each category, but we know that at least 100,000 men, women and children directly suffered, of whom about 1,000 were put to death.

Of course, while Slansky was the last target of Splinter Factor, he was not the last victim. There were more executions in Czechoslovakia in trials subsidiary to the Slansky trial. In East Germany distinguished members of the Central Committee who all had the misfortune to have known Noel Field were imprisoned. In Hungary there were daily arrests, secret trials and executions. In Poland they were still trying to break the will of Wladyslaw Gomulka and to this end they were arresting more people every day. In Rumania, Bulgaria and Albania the secret police, aided by Soviet advisers, went about rounding up the enemy, though, as Stalin's suspicion grew, no one knew from one day to the next who the enemy really was.

The madness reached Russia itself. Now that Zionism had become the major crime, the Jews of Russia faced each day with fear and each night with thanksgiving that thus far they had survived. On January 13, 1952, *Pravda* announced the arrest of a terrorist group of Jewish Kremlin doctors who, ever since 1945, had been steadily killing off the leadership one by one. Mass hysteria gripped the nation and the whole Communist bloc.

In Czechoslovakia the bodies of the eleven men who were executed were cremated. It was decided that there should be no burial place, no possible future shrine where a relative could leave flowers. The ashes were put into a potato sack and given to a driver of the security police to take out of Prague and bury in a field. But there was thick snow on the road, and the driver and the two men who came with him to dig the hole decided, after a few miles, that the journey was uncomfortable and senseless. So they stopped the car in a quiet road on the outskirts of the city, took out their sackful of ashes and sprinkled onto the icy surface the last earthly remains of the men who, but a short time before, had been their respected leaders.

EPILOGUE

His work completed, Lieutenant Colonel Jozef Swiatlo arrived in the West on December 21, 1953, two days before Beria's summary execution in Moscow. His story of his escape is a remarkable one. He told a Congressional committee in Washington that he was in East Berlin for a security conference with the Germans together with his chief, Anatol Fejgin.

> ... we had a little time, we wanted to see Berlin, and just by accident, through the underground railways, we found ourselves in West Berlin.
>
> At a certain moment, we didn't even realize that we were in West Berlin. We thought we were in the center of East Berlin. We realized we were in West Berlin ... when we went to some shop, and we had to pay the bill.

... We paid in the East German marks, and then the lady of the shop told us: "Gentlemen, you are in the western part of Berlin. Here we only accept Western marks."

Now, at that moment, I realized that to escape to West Berlin is no problem, but I also realized that the liking for the Western nice things of my chief was so great that if I ask him he would go again to Western Berlin, and indeed, the next day he went with me, on my initiative, to Western Berlin. . . . I planned it this way: When we had to exchange our Eastern marks for Western marks, we didn't do it together. First, I was to enter the place of exchange, and he would wait for me in the streets, since it wasn't very—well, formally—legal, and then he would enter the place for an exchange, and then I would have time to escape, and it happened exactly the way that I planned it the day before.

The day of my escape we went to the place of exchange. First I entered. I was there about five minutes. Then Fejgin entered, and I just left . . . [and] reported to the American authorities.

On another occasion, Swiatlo reported that Colonel Milka, the chief of security for East Berlin, had made this extraordinary journey with him. Both stories require a bit of believing. In all likelihood, he was "lifted" out by the CIA. It was none too soon, either. Stalin was dead, Beria had disappeared, the secret-police apparatus through the Soviet Union and Eastern Europe was crumbling. People were asking questions. It was time for a man with Swiatlo's record to leave.

In March 1954 Swiatlo suddenly was heard on Radio Free Europe. Night after night, in one of the most successful pieces of radio propaganda ever, he went on the air revealing to his appalled audience in Poland stories of how the Polish secret police operated. He named police inform-

ers in the factories and universities; he told how he had
arrested Gomulka and how other nationalist Communists
had been driven insane inside Polish prisons. He reported
that many Russians had worked with the Gestapo against
the Home Army during the war and that collaborators
were still members of the party and government.*

The effect was devastating. Though listening to RFE
broadcasts was illegal and though efforts were made to jam
the transmissions, all Poland heard Swiatlo with fascinated
horror. The government was forced to react—the stories
simply rang too true to be easily denied. Security men
began losing their jobs; ministers suddenly found power
slipping from them. No one could hide any more. The
nation was in ferment, and it all led to the Potsdam riots
and Gomulka's return to power.

In the meantime, of course, from the day Swiatlo
defected, a commission of experts sat down to disentangle
his files in an effort to pinpoint precisely what he knew and
what information he carried with him to the West. Slowly
at first, and then suddenly, the commission began to arrive
at the awful truth: Swiatlo had been working for the other
side all along.

But Swiatlo himself provided the clue as to the real
damage he had done. In a press conference in Washington
on September 28, 1954, on the day the U.S. attorney general announced that he had been given asylum in America,
Swiatlo told the world that the Fields were being held in
prison behind the Iron Curtain. Puzzled by his interest in
an affair long since forgotten, the commission examined the
Field file. It didn't take them long to come to the appropriate conclusions. The Fields were the innocent victims of a

---

* Swiatlo did not, of course, reveal that he himself had been playing a double role or that the Americans were responsible for some of
the terrible things that had occurred. To this day he will claim he was
an honest servant of the regime until he decided to defect to the West.

fearful plot. Embarrassed, the Polish government informed the Russians. Something had to be done.

On October 25, 1954, Hermann Field was told he was a free man. On November 19, after some necessary medical treatment in Warsaw, he finally caught the plane he had tried to depart on five years before. In his pocket was $40,000 compensation from the Polish government—the first case on record of a Communist government compensating a victim in cash for years of illegal detention.

On November 17 the Budapest radio announced that Noel and Herta Field had been released too. They met in a warder's office, their hair turned white by their terrible ordeal. He later wrote: "And now as the sobs well up, I know this is the most memorable moment in my life, bigger than happiness, bigger than sorrow. Through years of separation, we have remained one...."

They too were each given $40,000 in compensation and, astonishingly, chose to continue to live in Hungary. No one has ever adequately explained that decision, but perhaps they were told about Operation Splinter Factor and vowed never to return to an America which could abuse them so cruelly. Of course, the Communists had also committed inexcusable crimes against them. But the Fields were the kind of people who would regard the psychological torture inflicted by the U.S. more terrible than the physical torture they endured at the hands of the Communists.

Erica Wallach, who had been building roads in Siberia, had to wait a little longer. But on October 27, 1955, also with compensation money, she flew from Moscow to Berlin. The Field family, who had begun the whole affair so unwittingly, had at last all been accounted for.

Once the Fields had been officially declared innocent, cases of thousands of others throughout Eastern Europe had to be reviewed. Slowly the prisons opened, and out they came, blinking into the sunlight and filling their lungs with the breath of freedom.

Operation Splinter Factor, finally revealed to the East Europeans before Gomulka took power, had as its last fling direct responsibility for the Potsdam riots which were so dramatically to change modern Polish history. In June 1956, 30,000 Potsdam workers had permitted a strike to degenerate into the greatest demonstration ever against Soviet domination. Ever since then, the Polish government and party had sat in almost permanent crisis session. By October it was clear to the majority that only one man could hold the nation together, a man whose hands were clean and who, because of his courageous stance against the excesses of Stalinism, had become a popular hero to his people: the stern, unsmiling Wladyslaw Gomulka. Arrested in August 1951 and destined for the gallows, released in April 1956, he had been pitched from his prison cell into the seat of power. Gomulka's day had come, but it looked as though it would be a short one.

The huge Tupolev 104, which had been circling the city for an hour to give members of the Politburo time to get to the airport, swung down low over the tarmac and landed with a scream of jets and tires. A hastily summoned military guard of honor had drawn up to the saluting base and presented arms as a ramp was wheeled up to the now stationary plane and the great doors swung open.

The first man down the steps was Nikita Sergeevich Khrushchev. The date was October 19, 1956. The dawn had just begun to crack the dark skies open. The arrival of the Russians had been a surprise, so the Poles had been up for most of the night making a historic decision.

Khrushchev was shouting almost before his feet touched Polish soil. This was not the jocular, back-slapping, avuncular peasant leader who was charming his way from capital to capital. This was the Kremlin bully—brutal, evil-tempered and coarse. Nikita Sergeevich had arrived to set his house in order.

Though the Poles didn't yet know it, the Red Army was already on the march from its bases inside Poland and on the Polish border. The big tanks were rumbling toward the cities to underline Russian power. The only sign on that cold October morning was the phalanx of generals whom Khrushchev brought with him, all in full-dress uniform, medals gleaming on their chests. There was Marshal Konev, commander-in-chief of the Warsaw Pact forces, General Antonov, the Red Army chief of staff, and a dozen more.

The Soviet Praesidium was represented too, in order to apply the gentle art of political arm twisting. Khrushchev had brought his first team: Molotov, Mikoyan and Kaganovich. These were the men who believed they could have all of Poland for breakfast and still leave room for a hearty lunch.

"We shed our blood for this country and now they [the Poles] want to sell it to the Americans," Khrushchev screamed at nobody in particular.

A gray-faced, undernourished, pinched-looking man replied quietly. "We shed more blood than you and we're not selling out to anyone."

"Who is this man?" Khrushchev raged, his face mottled with fury.

"I am the former secretary-general of the party whom Stalin and you threw into prison. My name"—he drew himself up to his full height—"my name is Gomulka!"

"What is he doing here?" Khrushchev demanded, refusing to speak to Gomulka personally.

"He is here," replied another Pole, "because last night we elected him secretary-general of the party."

"Treason," Khrushchev exclaimed bitterly as he stepped into the car to drive him to Warsaw.

On his arrival in Warsaw, Khrushchev tried to force his way into the Central Committee, then meeting in plenary session, and demanded the removal of Gomulka and the election of a Politburo more to his liking. But his Polish hosts politely and firmly told him that he had not been invited.

Then came the bombshell. In the course of long and often bitter talks in Warsaw's Belvedere Palace, the Polish leaders were informed of Russian troop movements. In a hard, controlled voice, Gomulka turned on Khrushchev: "Unless the troops are called off at once, we will walk out of here and there will be no negotiations. We will not talk while cannons are pointing at Warsaw. Unless the troop movements are halted this instant, I, Wladyslaw Gomulka, will go on the Polish radio and tell the people what has happened here."

The radio station was told to stand by; trusted messengers went to the factories, the polytechnics, the schools and the universities. Quietly, the people put down their working tools and waited. Poland was ready to fight.

The Russians wavered. Their troops were halted. Gomulka was confirmed by the Central Committee as secretary-general and, forty-eight hours later, Khrushchev, now back in Moscow, cabled his congratulations. Poland, Wladyslaw Gomulka and, though Khrushchev didn't know it at the time, the Communist party had won.

A few days earlier, on October 6, another man, four hundred miles away in Budapest, had won a victory too. But there was a difference. Laszlo Rajk was dead. Some 300,000 Hungarians accompanied Rajk's widow and the entire Hungarian government to a cemetery in Budapest to honor with a solemn state funeral the man who had been brutally murdered almost exactly seven years before. But Rajk's spirit survived the man. His imprisonment had driven Hungary's yearning for freedom underground, and his death nourished the flame. Now it was to burst to the surface.

On the day that news of Gomulka's triumph reached Hungary, with emotions still high from the Rajk funeral, students, workers and soldiers marched to the statue of General Bem, the Polish hero of the 1848 revolution, where they sang the Marseillaise—as did the 1917 Bolshevik revolutionaries in Leningrad—and the Internationale. Soon the crowd grew to over 200,000; flags of the Communist party were burned, anti-Communist banners were held aloft, and Imre Nagy was lifted to power by the people. He spoke of free elections, of a return to the 1945 constitution, of Hungary being a neutral state and withdrawing from the Warsaw Pact. But here there was no Gomulka to stop the Russian tanks. They moved in and quelled by force what the world called the Hungarian Revolution.

In 1968, twelve years later, it was Czechoslovakia's turn. The bonds of a totalitarian state were snapped by its people: they demanded a freedom of choice and action which, in the view of the Kremlin, would almost certainly have eventually forced the Communist party out of power. This time it was Brezhnev and Kosygin who took the fateful decision, fully backed by Wladyslaw Gomulka, and Russian tanks were used again. The Czech spring was turned into an early winter.

Allen Dulles had been proved right. In the one country in Eastern Europe—Poland—where a nationalist Communist was still strong enough to seize power, the Communist party became more firmly entrenched than ever.

Gomulka had always been a Communist and could not conceive of a non-Communist Poland. Yet he wanted to provide a form of communism which suited the conditions of his own country, not one dictated by Moscow.

As Dulles had predicted, the presence of a nationalist Communist was not in the interest of the Western democracies if they wished to pry the satellites away from the warm embrace of Moscow. Gomulka gave the Poles a Communist government with which they could identify and which permitted them to face the future with some confidence. His second coming did not kill communism in Poland; it gave it renewed vigor and strength.

In Hungary and Czechoslovakia the purges had removed all those of Gomulka's caliber. Unlike the Poles, who perhaps for the first time in their history were prepared to settle for whatever they could get, the Hungarians and later the Czechs behaved precisely as Dulles said they would if Stalinist oppression removed all their important liberal leaders. They tried not merely to reform the party but to create a new one. When they spoke, as did the Czechs, of "socialism with a human face," they were speaking of a break with the Soviet Union. The Communist world, excluding so-called Communist China, is a system of governments, part of a vast interplay of economic, military and political forces, which has risen to power in Eastern Europe since the war and whose center of gravity is, and has to be, the Soviet Union. A Western-style democracy in one country of the bloc would have destroyed that solidarity.

This was, of course, what Allen Dulles was striving for. And he nearly succeeded. Splinter Factor failed only because the Russians were prepared to use all necessary force to cling to what they had. Whether Allen Dulles suspected that they might, we do not know. But in 1956, as

director of the CIA, he argued for Western intervention—
to finish off what he had begun—to liberate "the captive
nations" of Eastern Europe.

Members of a special CIA-trained army force, for-
eign-born nationals, stationed in Germany, were sent into
Hungary to help the revolutionaries. Radio Free Europe,
at that time controlled almost totally by the CIA, encouraged the Hungarian insurrectionists to hold on, for help
was at hand; the enemy were not the Russians but communism. On October 31 it broadcast: "The Ministry of
Defense and the Ministry of the Interior are still in Communist hands. Do not let this continue. Freedom fighters,
do not hang your weapons on the wall." It broadcast
instructions on how to make Molotov cocktails and encouraged revolution and insurrection. The Hungarians believed
it all, not realizing that RFE was speaking for itself and
the CIA and for no one else.

For the fact was, however heroic their struggle may
have seemed, no responsible Western leader could advocate
coming to the military assistance of either the Hungarians
or the Czechs—that would have meant World War III.

The future, in fact, looks bright. Communism is
changing. There is still oppression—only the brave dare
speak their mind and justice is not the automatic right of
all citizens. But the sheer violence which was done to the
human spirit in the forties and early fifties is becoming a
thing of the past. From here on the future can be faced
with a measure of optimism, for both Joseph Stalin and
Operation Splinter Factor, and the spirit which drove
them, are dead and buried. Of course, repression still exists
inside the Soviet Union, but the total criminal savagery
of Stalin's era is gone—one hopes for good.

Allen Dulles had forced a situation which only Russian tanks could put right. If that can be regarded as a suc-

cess, Allen Dulles triumphed indeed. But if the use of those tanks demonstrated how politics has become not an art at the service of the people but a science which the people must serve, then Operation Splinter Factor must go down in history as a malignant growth which totally disfigured the political integrity of our postwar world.

This book deals only with Czechoslovakia, Hungary, Poland and Bulgaria, and even then mentions only the most sensational trials. But there were hundreds of other trials, all over Eastern Europe, in which the Fields were directly involved and at which men were condemned to death or faced life imprisonment.

Once the truth was revealed, the families of the dead were able to comfort themselves with the knowledge that their fellow countrymen no longer officially regarded them as traitors or spies or saboteurs. The families of the living could get on with the task of picking up the pieces and starting all over again.

Hermann Field and his wife and Erica Wallach and her husband are today living normal lives in the United States, as is Jozef Swiatlo. Noel Field died two years ago, and his wife, Herta, lives in Budapest. Joseph Stalin is dead, and Klement Gottwald, who caught a chill at the funeral, died days later. Traicho Kostov, Laszlo Rajk and Rudolf Slansky have all had their names cleared, as have the men who shared the dock and their shame with them. Wladyslaw Gomulka was deposed in 1971, his political arteries hardened by age. Allen Dulles left the CIA in 1961, after the Bay of Pigs debacle, and died in 1969.

But they are all men of the past. Tomorrow belongs to another generation.

POSTSCRIPT

At face value, an operation to remove from office all the liberal-minded Communists in Eastern Europe in order to force the people to discover the reality of Communist rule—education through suffering—appears to have something to recommend it. But even if it were desirable to interfere in the internal affairs of sovereign states in this way, such a scenario does not stand up to a moment's examination.

It is, of course, true that the Polish "events of 1956" —as the buildup to Gomulka's return to power is called— and the Hungarian Revolution give some support to the thesis that the people of a country bereft of all natural leaders must eventually rise up in revolt in order to achieve their political goals. But two points cannot be disregarded. First, Polish and Hungarian uprisings occurred after the process of liberalization had already begun, a fact which of itself denies the Dulles theory that people will rebel only after they have been driven to a state of total despair. The opposite is the truth. Only hope can breed hope. Stalinism and the Stalinist terror machine produced a state of political apathy; the peoples of Eastern Europe came alive again only after Khrushchev had begun on his process of de-Stalinization. The Russians faced the dilemma then, and they face it today perhaps even more strongly: introduce some freedoms, and the people will demand more; grant them their demands and they will demand more again. Operation Splinter Factor managed to retard this process by many years, and that is perhaps the most damaging indictment which one can make of it. Second—a point apparently not originally realized by the authors of the plan—the Russian government did not regard their Eastern European possessions merely as a piece of real estate; they were and are essential to their defense planning and to their notions of security.

President Roosevelt understood Stalin's obsession with the need to protect forever the sanctity of Russian borders. Perhaps if he had lived, Stalin would have been satisfied that countries like Czechoslovakia and Hungary could be allies and not colonies. But that was not to be the case. Once the satellites became so transformed, once they became an interlocking part of the military mechanism of the Warsaw Pact, then Russia, if necessary, was prepared to fight or intervene to keep them in line. Instead of encouraging this possibility, it should have been the first object of Western policy makers to encourage the growth of pro-Communist, pro-Russian but independent sovereign governments in all of the countries of Eastern Europe (to prop up, for example, the Communist-dominated coalition government which came to power in Hungary after rela-

tively free elections in November 1945)—and not, as did
Allen Dulles, help to destroy them. The Russian invasion
of Hungary in 1956 and of Czechoslovakia in 1968 were two
of the most tragic events of postwar European history. But
in each case Russia was faced not merely with loss of
empire, which would have been serious enough, but with
the dismemberment of its entire strategic posture on the
geopolitical/military map of Europe.

That, rather than the fact of invasion, was the real
tragedy. It was for military rather than political reasons
that the counterrevolution in those two countries had to
be squashed. For by the time they revolted, they had
ceased to be nations; they had become instead mere military flanks.

The responsibility for that state of affairs, which made
the subsequent brutal Russian intervention inevitable,
does not rest solely with the Soviet government. It must
also be shared by the authors of Operation Splinter Factor,
who increased rather than diminished the Soviet hold on
these countries; who shored up the authority of the Stalinists; who heightened Soviet fear and suspicion of the Western allies; and who, because of all of that, helped impose
upon the nations of Eastern Europe a colonial status
which quite possibly could have been avoided.

So Stalin, led blindly into the Splinter Factor trap,
turned Eastern Europe into a mere extension of the Soviet
Union, ruled by the unscrupulous power of the secret
police. The possibility of dialogue across the barrier of the
Iron Curtain was reduced to zero, and two mighty blocs
became frozen in their deadly resolve one day to destroy
one another.

It would be foolish to pretend that Operation Splinter
Factor caused the Cold War. But it did unquestionably
give it that special tone of savage, all-consuming beastli-

ness which was so much the hallmark of that era. It took the Cold War and all but turned it into a Hot War. It destroyed the dreams of a generation and made the world a safer place for its secret police.

Operation Splinter Factor destroyed any hope of a genuine political dialogue between the governor and the governed in Eastern Europe for years to come, and it poisoned the relations of these countries with Russia and with each other.

As for the West, where Allen Dulles's own constituents lived and on whose behalf all of this was done, it too was led down a blind alley from which it is only now beginning to escape. We, too—though most of us did not realize it—were victims of a subtle propaganda machine which stunted our political development and which has led to recent tragedies like the Vietnam War.

It took Vietnam to teach Americans that they did not have a God-given right to interfere in the internal affairs of another country; that they were not obliged to correct social systems different from their own; and that they could actually live in peace with a nation which has a system of government different from their own. It took Vietnam to show us that of the two alternatives—learning to live with Communists and fighting Communists—the first is quite preferable to the second. Now that President Nixon has actually visited Communist China, it is easier to see how barren American and British foreign policy was during the early days of the Cold War.

This is not to say that they were dealing with an easy adversary or to pretend that Stalin was the misunderstood good guy of postwar international affairs. But what was so astonishing about American policy was that it was based on fear and uncertainty. Here was the richest nation the world had ever seen, a nation which contained all the talents and the greatest of virtues, a nation which emerged from the war with both power and prestige and yet which despite all of that responded to the challenge of world leadership like a frightened boy on his first day at school. America behaved as if she were assailed by an enemy so mighty that she was fighting for her life. The Cold War began and lasted so long because two powerful nation states entered the second half of the twentieth century loaded down by a massive sense of inferiority. The Russians had some cause, but America had none.

Politically counterproductive, unnecessarily barbarous and unquestionably a failure, Operation Splinter Factor was part of that bleak period. It lies as an ugly stain upon the honor and integrity of the United States and must rank as one of the darkest chapters in the whole history of American diplomacy and espionage.

One cannot research a book of this nature without wondering whether operations of similar scale and scope are under way today. Unfortunately, one has no way of knowing. If black was capable of being turned into white in the forties, then white can be turned into black today. Neither can one talk to intelligence men about a subject like Operation Splinter Factor without at one point feeling oneself to be part of some enormous fantasy. Surely, one thinks, people don't really behave like this.

It is unworthy of our democracy to shuffle off all responsibility onto agencies like the CIA or SIS. The directors and staffs of these agencies are the servants of the people. They operate within the guidelines we, through our elected representatives, give them. If it seems that they consistently stray beyond them, we, through our elected representatives, must insist that they be punished. The trouble is that our elected representatives are rather too lax when it comes to exercising proper control. In America, Britain, France and Germany the security agencies have become states within states, virtually autonomous units operating at a level which precludes any direct executive control over their actions. They are not to blame if the systems of accountability have broken down. It is we who are at fault; we have not insisted often enough and loudly enough that the controls which exist should be constantly reinforced and that where they do not exist they should be immediately introduced.

Nor is it right to blame the agencies for the weapons they employ to fight their secret war. It is we who arm them. And if we, for fear of offending our sense of morality, do not inquire closely as to how these weapons are used, then we have no right to criticize if we subsequently discover the horrible uses to which they have been put. We are all put off too easily from making our inquiries because we are told the national interest is involved. Yet what the national interest is at any one period of our history must be a political decision in which all of us, if we live in a democracy, have the duty to inform ourselves about and seek to influence. Instead of the term being a cloak behind which the executive branch can hide, it should be the very cornerstone upon which it has been elected to office.

The national interest of the great Western democracies is not hard to define. It must surely be to prove by example to Communist and non-Communist countries alike that our Western democracy is a superior form of government which enshrines within its basic fabric universal truths such as freedom, humanity, legality and equality.

It is of course hard to use these principles as weapons when one is fighting an unscrupulous foe. Yet surely if one seeks to defend democracy by using the weapons of totalitarianism, one has lost the battle before the first shot has been fired. Operation Splinter Factor has shown how deeply the foreign policies of a nation can be contaminated by the premise that a just cause often needs to be pursued by unjust means. No higher or more sublime duty now faces our leaders and those of us who elect them than to ensure that this philosophy of desperation is erased forever from our way of life. It is too fragile to bear the strain much longer.

NOTES ON SOURCES

The springboard for my research was the work of that fine American journalist Flora Lewis. In her book *The Man Who Disappeared*, which brilliantly traced the tragic history of Noel Field, she wrote:

> A certain jauntiness of spirit, induced by the intriguing job ahead, launched me on the collector's trail.
>
> It did not last long. First went confident requests to American, Swiss, French, British and German intelligence centers whose files on Field could no longer reasonably be on the active, highly secret list since the people involved had all long since been exposed. The answers that came back were startling. Some were polite, some gruff and resentful even of the query. All made plain that the old reports on the tracks Noel Field had

left around the world were still in the highly sensitive category. As a newspaperwoman who had worked in many countries, I knew enough people involved or connected with intelligence agencies to send the requests through correct and respected channels.

I was surprised at the blanket rejection, and I tried again in other ways. Discreetly but firmly, the answer came back. It was no.

On the face of it, there was no logic in the refusal. Inevitably I wondered why plain questions of dates and places that must have been on record were still secret; why I was flatly refused access to a communist defector [Swiatlo] living in the United States who could know only the communist side of the case and who had been permitted to publish and broadcast at length great chunks of his knowledge when the Field case was still open. . . . Then I was told bluntly and with overtones of warning that it had nothing to do with me, that there were "reasons" for keeping the dossiers locked and that it would be taken badly if I insisted on trying to break through the official barrier of silence.*

Despite an enormous research program, Miss Lewis was never able to find out the real reason why Field was arrested or why that "barrier of silence" existed. Nor did she know why there was still so much nervousness surrounding the case or why, as she says, "most of the people who saw me and told me what they knew, or told me of others who might know something, did so on condition that they not be named as sources."

Nevertheless, I plugged myself into Miss Lewis's book and her research material. So thoroughly did she cover the territory that I quickly realized it would be a waste of effort to tramp around the same course myself. That per-

* Flora Lewis, *The Man Who Disappeared* (London: Arthur Barker Ltd., 1965), pp. 16, 17.

mitted me to concentrate my energies and resources on the
Splinter Factor operation itself, leaving the Field saga very
much to her.

However, all the difficulties she encountered in writing
her book I encountered a thousandfold, for it quickly
became apparent to people who were willing to help me initially that I had hit upon something which it was in no
one's interest to have revealed. I found, as did Miss Lewis,
that those able to help did so only on the condition that I
not reveal my source. Those willing, and perhaps wanting,
to be named knew nothing of any significance. Certainly
no one is going to talk about recent intelligence operations
unless he is assured that, whatever else happens, his ano-
nymity will be preserved. My journalistic training in handling similar problems helped me first of all to make contact
with people in senior positions who were told by go-
betweens that I could be, and had been in the past, trusted.
Secondly, having worked in the area of nonattribution for
so long, I was particularly well qualified to separate truth
from fiction; I applied rigid criteria in judging nonattrib-
utable information and I believe I managed to minimize
the risk of swallowing propaganda.

There were four distinct categories of sources:

1. Former members of the CIA. These passed me one
to the other, like a baton in a relay race, until I eventually
hit upon a few people who were not only prepared to help
but who believed that, since this whole affair was so far in
the past, the public should at last understand something
about the Cold War, which has shaped all of our lives. This
public-spiritedness, understandably perhaps, has not
extended to any desire to see their names in print. Months
after I met one of them, I telephoned him in Switzerland
and asked permission to use his name. He had long since
left the agency and was well established in his own right

with surely nothing to fear. He not only pleaded with me
not to do so but literally took the next plane to London to
reinforce his objections in person.

2. Past members of Eastern European security services and armies who have defected to the West. They were
difficult to contact and prime for information, since most
live in terror, believing that the KGB will one day ring at
their front doors and take its revenge. To name them would
be unforgivable—not necessarily because the Russians
would come hunting but because they would fear such an
eventuality.

3. Current employees of government and governmental organizations in the West. I received much useful background information from these people, who, of course, risk
losing their jobs if their identities are divulged.

4. Current employees of governments in the East
European bloc. I must say I was very surprised that they
desired to remain anonymous and cooperated to a lesser
extent than I had originally been led to expect. I learned
that functionaries in Eastern Europe are terrified by their
dealings with Western journalists and authors. They are
afraid of being blamed for interpretations of their statements with which their governments may not agree and of
being held responsible for sections of the book which are
regarded as hostile, whether or not these were discussed
with them.

When approached by a go-between, Jozef Swiatlo initially took a benevolent attitude toward this work and
accepted the general premises upon which it is based. It
was he who corrected my original information—that this
was a British rather than an American operation. However, though he himself has little to be ashamed of, subsequent attempts to contact him either officially, through

the Community Office of the State Department, or unofficially, failed. A security curtain had been drawn around him.

Though Hermann Field knew nothing of the real reasons why he spent so many years in prison, his story is a fascinating one. While his memory was still fresh and his emotions, as a result of his release, alive, he was interviewed for the internal purposes of Radio Free Europe (and presumably interested agencies) by a Mr. A. Blazynski on March 20, 1955—four months after his return to the West.

The Blazynski report is still a confidential document inside RFE. In a commentary at the end, Blazynski wrote:

> ... there can be detected in his answers and questions a certain naïveté and amazement. How could it all have happened? How was he to be used against anyone else and especially against people he did not even know? When I recalled his official role in the Slansky trial and in the purges of East German Communists he was visibly surprised and taken aback. He knew nothing about this.

The importance of this material for me was that it contained the thoughts of an innocent victim of Splinter Factor as he was at the time, not as he feels now, after several years have passed.

In this respect, Swiatlo also left a valuable trail. The broadcasts I refer to in the text are from the archives of RFE, and though in some cases Swiatlo managed to twist the facts sufficiently to present a case rather than speak the literal truth, they comprise an enormous and most important record of the man himself and the political

system which bred him. Using an ex-colleague of Swiatlo's
as my guide through a massive volume of transcripts, I
have relied upon these broadcasts as a backdrop to my
researches.

The last days of Rudolf Slansky are admirably if somewhat emotionally recorded by Madame Slanska in her own
story, originally published in Czechoslovakia in 1968. I
have the advantage of being well acquainted with a friend
of the family who was able to indicate for me passages in
the book where a wife's devotion and loyalty to her husband permitted her to see events which did not quite occur
the way she describes them. Still, she writes of her own
experiences with remarkable objectivity.

With regard to the Czech material as a whole, I am
especially indebted to one source. Karel Kaplan, the distinguished Czech historian, is, I understand, currently serving
a prison sentence for misusing the official archives. During
Dubcek's brief reign, he managed to get permission to
examine the papers relating to the Slansky case in the
archives of the Communist party's Central Committee and
the Ministry of the Interior. As a result, he managed to
write an astonishing 30,000-word treatise about the trials,
about the political and international atmosphere which led
to them and about how the nation in particular and the
Eastern bloc in general became so completely mesmerized
by Joseph Stalin. The Kaplan papers were published
briefly (and then withdrawn from circulation) in *Nova
Mysl (New Thought)*, an academic periodical, and went
virtually unnoticed in the West. In fact, they comprise one
of the most remarkable documents ever written by a Communist historian about events in his own country.

I managed to secure the complete papers through a
distinguished Czech *émigré* in Amsterdam and had them
privately translated. The problem, of course, is that Mr.

Kaplan may well suffer renewed deprivations because of
the use I have made of his work. However, I feel sure that
he would wish his papers to receive the widest attention,
which they unquestionably deserve. Equally, I feel that by
drawing attention to his plight, I may prompt fellow historians to protest in the most vehement way possible the
treatment currently being meted out to this distinguished
man. Although I am familiar with the Piller Commission
Report on the trials, I regard Kaplan's work as far superior.
(As it is possible that I have the only English translation,
I will be pleased to make it available to scholars of the
period.)

Eugen Loebl, once a fellow defendant of Slansky's and
a Czechoslovak minister, and now teaching international
affairs at an American university, was a most valuable
source on the political implications of the trials and the
psychology of the era. This brave and brilliant man, who
suffered so greatly and yet is unmarked by bitterness, provided me with a philosophical understanding of an era that
I lived through as a mere child. After two long seminars
with him, I felt I was beginning to comprehend the motiva-
tions of the principal participants in the Splinter Factor
story, and this understanding made the mechanics of
writing the book possible.

The name of the intelligence operation, Splinter
Factor, has never before been published. However, after I
had completed my book I learned that the American writer
Robert Deindorfer is due to publish the memoirs of an ex-
officer of Britain's Secret Intelligence Service, in which not
only is the operation featured but its name is revealed.
Upon hearing of my work, Mr. Deindorfer was clearly concerned that readers might assume he took the operational
name from this book. This is not the case, and I am glad,
from both our points of view, to confirm that we discovered

the operational title Splinter Factor quite independently of each other.

In Chapter 1 the Sullivan material came from a former employee of the CIA who was on the inside track of Operation Splinter Factor from its very beginnings and who personally knew Sullivan. I have made extensive use of existing literature on Soviet espionage practice: Otto Heilbrunn's excellent *The Soviet Secret Services*, Boris Levytsky's *The Uses of Terror: The Soviet Secret Service 1917–1970* and Ronald Hingley's *The Russian Secret Police;* and on Western espionage practice: Christopher Felix's *The Spy and His Masters* and David Wise's and Thomas B. Ross's *The Espionage Establishment*. I had also done a great deal of original research among past operatives of the CIA, SIS and the Russian security services as to modern espionage terminology and practice. Like all professions, spying has its own jargon which crosses international frontiers. As one former SIS man told me, "I feel I have more in common with my Soviet adversaries than I do with my neighbors in Surrey." It's a point of view shared by most of the professionals.

In Chapter 2 the story of Jozef Swiatlo's early years comes from his testimony in October 1954 to the House Select Committee to Investigate Communist Aggression and the Forced Incorporation of the Baltic States into the USSR. All the information in Chapter 3 is new and comes from sources within SIS.

In Chapter 4 the material on Allen Dulles's role in securing the surrender of Italian troops has been told by himself in *The Craft of Intelligence* and has been covered by wartime historians; the quotations from Stalin and Roosevelt come from official American records of the period. The report of the conversation between Dulles and

Prince Hohenlohe, which comes from East German archives and was first quoted in a pamphlet by Bob Edwards, M.P., and Kenneth Dunne entitled *A Study of a Master Spy*, has been the subject of controversy. In actual fact it had been rewritten by Soviet propagandists as part of a "disinformation" campaign against Dulles. The record of the original conversation is available among the captured German papers, Series T-120, German Foreign Office, in the National Archives, Washington, D.C. While Dulles's immediate postwar career is shrouded in some mystery, few experts who have studied the subject doubt that he was an active intelligence agent. Dulles's own view that he would become the director of the CIA immediately upon Dewey's inauguration is, I believe, told for the first time here but is no secret inside the intelligence community.

In Chapter 5 the material on Noel Field's life has been most admirably and sensitively chronicled by Flora Lewis in *The Man Who Disappeared*. The trial of Alger Hiss produced interesting information relating to Hede Massing. Needless to say, there are no records available to journalists on the details of the Splinter Factor conspiracy, and accordingly all matters relating to it come from personal interviews of people then involved in it. Similarly, I pieced together the information in Chapter 6 from interviews I conducted over a period of years with former members of the CIA and SIS whose names cannot be revealed.

In Chapter 7 the material on the disappearance of the Field family was drawn from accounts in the above-mentioned book by Flora Lewis; press accounts from the period (principally in the London *Daily Telegraph* and *The New York Times*); interviews with people in Eastern Europe; and the Czech Piller Commission Report. The information about Erica Glaser Wallach comes largely from her testimony on March 21, 1958, to the House Committee on

Un-American Activities. I had access to the full testimony, as distinct from the edited version, which was published.

Details of the arrest of Noel Field in Chapter 8 have been published in Czech official documents available to historians in 1968. I have relied extensively on Professor Karel Kaplan's researches and also on the Piller Commission Report into the Slansky trials as edited by Jiri Pelikan. The report of the meeting of the Central Committee of the Polish Communist party in 1956, freely available in Poland, produced Jakub Berman's version of events. The report of Rajk's arrest comes from members of his family and from details available in Hungary during the Hungarian Revolution and brought out, though not in documentary form, by Hungarian refugees.

The details of the Rajk trial in Chapter 9 have been drawn from the recollections of Hungarians at the time, but largely from the English-language transcript of the trial published in Budapest in 1949 under the title "Laszlo Rajk and His Accomplices Before the People's Court." The transcript was, in fact, issued throughout the world as a piece of pro-Soviet propaganda.

The material on Kostov in Chapter 10 comes from Bulgarian newspapers of the period and also from published documents of the Bulgarian Central Committee. The Kostov trial record also derives from contemporary references in the Bulgarian press and from the *British Daily Worker*, which from the beginning had a correspondent, Anne Kelly, attending the trial and covering the case extensively. The Gomulka case was pieced together from references in the Polish press, from Radio Free Europe transcripts of Jozef Swiatlo's broadcast to Poland from Munich in March 1954, and also from his unpublished, undated typescript in the archives of Radio Free Europe, "The Inside Story of the Bezpieka and the Party."

A major reassessment of the Korean War, its causes and effects is currently being carried out in the Research and Analysis Department of the State Department. Chapter 11 is based upon interviews with a researcher in that section. The Acheson-Truman papers on the Korean War are still locked away in the archives, and until they are released no serious study of this war will be possible. Oddly enough, more is known today about Vietnam than the war which preceded it by so many years.

The Czechoslovak trials described in Chapters 12 through 14 have been well documented. On a personal level, men like Artur London and Eugen Loebl wrote books about their own trials and imprisonment, and both have significant things to say about Rudolf Slansky. Madame Slanska has outlined in her *Report on My Husband* the events leading to the arrest and the arrest itself. On an official level, Professor Kaplan's writings and the Piller Commission Report fill in the remaining gaps with quite astonishing revelations of the debates going on behind closed doors among members of the party and the government, including Stalin's personal intervention. The trial itself was given extensive coverage in the press at the time, but the best verbatim report is to be found in Eugen Loebl's book *Sentenced and Tried*. The macabre scattering of the ashes is described by Professor Kaplan.

The Swiatlo quote in the Epilogue comes from his testimony to the House Select Committee to Investigate Communist Aggression as well as from a press conference he held in New York on September 28, 1954, as reported in *The New York Times* and the *Daily Telegraph*. The Budapest radio announcement concerning the Fields' release comes from the files of Radio Free Europe, and Erica Wallach's release is described in her testimony to the Committee on Un-American Activities. The account of Khrushchev's arrival in Warsaw on October 19 comes from contemporary press reports in the London *Times* and *The New York Times* and from Flora Lewis's book *The Polish Volcano*. It has also been filled out with interviews with Polish diplomats in Warsaw at the time.

BIBLIOGRAPHY

Alperovitz, Gar. *Atomic Diplomacy: Hiroshima and Potsdam.* London: Martin Secker & Warburg Ltd., 1966.

Armstrong, John A. *The Politics of Totalitarianism: The Communist Party of the Soviet Union from 1934 to the Present.* New York: Random House, Inc., 1961.

——. *Soviet Partisans in World War II.* Madison, Wis.: University of Wisconsin Press, 1964.

Beck, F. [pseud.], and Godin, W. [pseud.]. *Russian Purge and the Extraction of Confession.* London: Hurst & Blackett, Ltd., 1951.

Cary, William H. *Poland Struggles Forward.* New York: Greenberg, 1949.

Chambers, Whittaker. *Witness.* London: André Deutsch Ltd., 1953.

Conquest, Robert. *Power and Policy in the U.S.S.R.: The Study of Soviet Dynastics.* London: Macmillan & Co. Ltd., 1961.

————, ed. *The Soviet Police System*. London: The Bodley Head Ltd., 1968.

Cookridge, E. H. *Gehlen, Spy of the Century*. New York: Random House, 1972.

Dallin, David J. *Soviet Espionage*. New Haven: Yale University Press, 1955.

Deacon, Richard. *The Russian Secret Service*. London: Frederick Muller Ltd., 1972.

Dedijer, Vladimir. *Tito Speaks: His Self-Portrait and Struggle with Stalin*. London: George Weidenfeld & Nicolson, Ltd. 1953.

Deutscher, Isaac. *Stalin: A Political Biography*. London: Oxford University Press, 1967.

Dewar, Hugo. *The Modern Inquisition*. London: Allan Wingate Ltd., 1953.

Djilas, Milovan. *Conversations with Stalin*. London: Rupert Hart-Davis Ltd., 1962.

Donnelly, Desmond. *Struggle for the World: The Cold War from Its Origins in 1917*. London: William Collins Sons & Co. Ltd., 1965.

Dulles, Allen. *The Craft of Intelligence*. London: George Weidenfeld & Nicolson, 1963.

Edwards, Robert, and Dunne, Kenneth. *A Study of a Master Spy*. London: Housemans, 1961.

Fainsod, Merle. *How Russia Is Ruled*. Cambridge, Mass.: Harvard University Press, 1963.

Felix, Christopher [pseud.]. *The Spy and His Masters*. London: Martin Secker & Warburg Ltd., 1963.

Field, Hermann, and Mierzenski, Stanislaw. *Angry Harvest*. New York: Thomas Y. Crowell, 1958.

Field, Noel. "Hitching Our Wagon to a Star." *Mainstream* magazine, January 1961.

Fontaine, André. *History of the Cold War*. 2 vols. London: Martin Secker & Warburg Ltd., 1970.

Foote, Alexander [pseud.]. *Handbook for Spies*. London: Museum Press Ltd., 1949.

Gehlen, Reinhard. *The Service.* New York: World Publishing Co., 1972.

Grey, Ian. *The First Fifty Years: Soviet Russia, 1917–1967.* London: Hodder & Stoughton Ltd., 1967.

Heilbrunn, Otto. *The Soviet Secret Services.* London: George Allen & Unwin Ltd., 1956.

Hingley, Ronald. *The Russian Secret Police.* London: Hutchinson & Co. Ltd., 1970.

Hiscocks, Richard. *Poland, Bridge for the Abyss?* London: Oxford University Press, 1963.

Hiss, Alger. *In the Court of Public Opinion.* New York: Alfred A. Knopf, Inc., 1957.

Hohne, Heinz, and Zolling, Herman. *The General Was a Spy: The True Story of General Gehlen and His Spy Ring.* New York: Coward, McCann & Geoghegan, Inc., 1972.

Howe, Quincy. *Ashes of Victory: World War II and Its Aftermath.* New York: Simon and Schuster, 1972.

Kempton, Murray. *Part of Our Time: Some Ruins and Monuments of the Thirties.* New York: Simon and Schuster, 1955.

Kimche, Jon. *Spying for Peace: General Guisan and Swiss Neutrality.* London: George Weidenfeld & Nicolson, Ltd. 1961.

Kirkpatrick, Lyman B., Jr. *The Real CIA.* New York: The Macmillan Co., 1968.

Lane, Arthur Bliss. *I Saw Freedom Betrayed.* London: Regency Publications, Ltd., 1949.

"Laszlo Rajk and His Accomplices Before the People's Court." Budapest: 1949.

Levytsky, Boris. *The Uses of Terror: The Soviet Secret Service 1917–70.* London: Sidgwick & Jackson Ltd., 1971.

Lewis, Flora. *The Man Who Disappeared: The Strange History of Noel Field.* London: Arthur Barker Ltd., 1966.

———. *The Polish Volcano: A Case History of Hope.* London: Martin Secker & Warburg Ltd., 1965.

Livre Blanc sur les procédés agressifs des gouvernements de l'URSS, de Pologne, de Tchecoslovaquie, de Hongrie, de Roumanie, de Bulgarie et d'Albanie envers la Yougoslavie Belgrade: 1951.

Loebl, Eugen. *Sentenced and Tried.* London: Elek Books Ltd., 1969.

London, Artur. *L'Aveu.* Paris: Gallimard, 1968.

——. *On Trial.* London: Macdonald & Co., 1970.

Lonsdale, Gordon. *Spy: Twenty Years of Secret Service.* London: Neville Spearman, 1965.

Luard, Evan, ed. *The Cold War—A Reappraisal.* London: Thames & Hudson Ltd., 1964.

Marchenko, Anatoly. *My Testimony.* London: Pall Mall Press Ltd., 1969.

Massing, Hede. *This Deception.* New York: Duell, Sloan & Pearce, Inc., 1951.

Moore, Barrington, *Terror and Progress USSR: Some Sources of Change and Stability in the Soviet Dictatorship.* London: Oxford University Press, 1954.

Payne, Robert. *The Rise and Fall of Stalin.* London: Pan Books Ltd., 1968.

Pelikan, Jiri, ed. *The Czechoslovak Political Trials 1950–1954.* London: Macdonald & Co., 1971.

Penkovsky, Oleg V. *The Penkovsky Papers.* London: William Collins & Co. Ltd., 1965.

Philby, Kim. *My Silent War.* London: Macgibbon & Kee Ltd., 1965.

Polish Central Committee. *Report on the Eighth Plenum.* Warsaw: State Publishing House, 1956.

Rauch, Georg von. *A History of Soviet Russia.* London: Thames & Hudson Ltd., 1957.

Rigby, T. H., ed. *The Stalin Dictatorship: Khrushchev's Secret Speech and Other Documents.* London: Methuen & Co. Ltd., 1968.

Schapiro, Leonard. *The Government and Politics of the Soviet Union.* London: Hutchinson & Co. Ltd., 1965.

Seton-Watson, Hugh. *The East European Revolution.* London: Methuen & Co. Ltd., 1950.

———. *From Lenin to Malenkov: The History of World Communism*. New York: Frederick A. Praeger, 1953.

Slanska, Josefa. *Report on My Husband*. London: Hutchinson & Co. Ltd., 1969.

Smith, R. Harris. *OSS: The Secret History of America's First Central Intelligence Agency*. Berkeley, Calif.: University of California Press, 1972.

Swiatlo, Jozef. "The Inside Story of the Bezpieka and the Party." Unpublished.

Szasz, Bela. *Volunteers for the Gallows*. London: Chatto & Windus Ltd., 1971.

The Trial of Nikola D. Petkov. Record of the Judicial Proceedings. Sofia: 1947.

The Trial of Rudolf Slansky and Others. Transcript of Prague Radio Broadcasts from files of Radio Free Europe.

The Trial of Traicho Kostov. Transcript. Sofia: 1949.

Tully, Andrew. *Central Intelligence Agency*. London: Arthur Barker Ltd., 1962.

U.S. Congress. House Committee on Un-American Activities. Testimony of Whittaker Chambers, August 27, 1948.

———. House Committee on Un-American Activities. Testimony of Erica Wallach, March 1958.

———. House Select Committee to Investigate Communist Aggression and the Forced Incorporation of the Baltic States into the USSR. Testimony of Josef Swiatlo, October 1954.

Weintal, Edward, and Bartlett, Charles. *Facing the Brink: A Study of Crisis Diplomacy*. London: Hutchinson & Co. Ltd., 1967.

Wise, David, and Ross, Thomas B. *The Espionage Establishment*. London: Jonathan Cape, Ltd., 1967.

———. *The Invisible Government*. London: Jonathan Cape, Ltd., 1965.

Wolfe, Bertram D. *Khrushchev and Stalin's Ghost: Text, Background and Meaning of Khrushchev's Secret Report to the Twentieth Congress on the Night of February 24–25, 1956*. London: Atlantic Press, 1957.

INDEX